SWEET
SUCCESS

SWEET SUCCESS

12 PROVEN HABITS OF WINNING LEADERS

BILL BYRD

WITH LARRY K. WEEDEN

Fleming H. Revell

A Division of Baker Book House Co
Grand Rapids, Michigan 49516

Published by Fleming H. Revell
a division of Baker Book House Company
P.O. Box 6287, Grand Rapids, MI 49516-6287
www.bakerbooks.com

Printed in the United States of America

Library of Congress Cataloging-in-Publication Data
Byrd, Bill, 1943-
    Sweet success : 12 proven habits of winning leaders / Bill Byrd
    with Larry K. Weeden.
        p.   cm.
    ISBN 0-8007-1844-5
    1. Success : I. Weeden, Larry K. II. Title.
    BJ1611.2.B97 2004
    158′.4—dc22   2003019450

The names of some individuals described in this book have been changed to protect their privacy.

BILL BYRD'S
SWEET SUCCESS

Best known for building the Sweet Shop Fudge Love Chocolate Factory in Fort Worth, Texas, from 1977 to 1992, entrepreneur Bill Byrd learned the leadership habits in this book the way many folks experience but rarely listen to—from hard work and many mistakes. He owned and operated the company for over fifteen years, and it has since been established as one of the largest hand-dipped-chocolate factory in America.

Byrd has since launched a small sandwich counter at a Fort Worth mall, a full-service restaurant called Mimi's, and a medical pool that helps physicians find and establish new offices.

Any business can be a good one, he believes, when a leader is most interested in touching the lives of colleagues, employees, customers, and students. That's why, along the road to success, he's dabbled in a celebrity-driven restaurant, a limousine service, and a business brokerage firm—each confirming his belief that business ought to begin and end with helping people.

5

Byrd continues to build up companies from a Ma and Pa scale and has run candy companies, ice cream franchises, and even a women's fashion shop. Today he and his wife, Judie, run the Culinary School of Fort Worth; she teaches as he develops new programs and systems.

Ever entrepreneurial, his first ventures—running a home business of TV repair and raising calves for feed-lots—began as he finished his master's in psychology and earned a bachelor's degree in electronics and math-ematics. He taught both high school electronics and math, then served as a county coordinator for vocational education, placing high school and college students in jobs throughout the community.

His reputation began there as a successful business-man who loves people; he's advised and coached others with marriage, family, and personal issues ever since. He frequently mentors colleagues and new entrepre-neurs. In church, he's served as an elder for thirteen years, and with Judie he's taught a class for newlywed couples.

As a founding board member of Emmaus Christian School in Mexico, he helped establish a school that started with four students and now houses and instructs 350 children from impoverished areas, giving them a first opportunity for formal education.

Whatever the enterprise of the moment, Byrd says his foremost job and finest hours are in his role as dad to his three children and granddad to his four grandkids: "Spending one-on-one time with them is what gets me out of bed in the morning."

Whether running an international corporation, lead-ing his family in prayer at dinnertime, or playfully leading a conga line to the tune of their own composition ("Shadrach, Meshach, and Abednego"), Byrd defines the sweetest success this way: loving and being loved by God, knowing and being known by his children and wife, and helping others.

CONTENTS

CONTENTS

ACKNOWLEDGMENTS

My thanks must go first to my mother, Lucille Byrd, who modeled faithfulness her entire life, never wavering in her commitment to her children.

The support of my family—my wife, Judie, and children, Teresa, Brian, and David—is indispensable. They truly are the most important part of my life on this earth. Judie's love and patience have been constant through all the ups and downs of my entrepreneurial journey, often with no paycheck on the horizon, yet always without hesitation or complaint. Our children were my primary reason for doing this book, hoping that they and their kids could learn from my experiences and not have to repeat all my mistakes.

My friend Bill Hendricks was the first professional writer to look at my notes and say I definitely had a message worth publishing. His encouragement kept me going!

Through this project I've made a new friend in Larry Weeden. His understanding and wordsmithing ability helped me tremendously in shaping my thoughts into readable prose.

My editor, Jeanette Thomason, had faith in the book and gave me the chance to put my message in print. For that I will always be grateful.

Finally, Leslie Nunn Reed, my agent and publicist, believed in this book from the beginning. She played a vital part in finding a home for it and getting it launched. She, too, deserves many thanks.

INTRODUCTION

WHY YOU NEED THIS BOOK

In a rapidly changing world, with perpetually uncertain economic times and increasing global competition, today's leader needs more than theory about what practices ought to work. He or she needs tried and proven counsel from someone who has been meeting payrolls and making businesses thrive in good times and bad for decades.

Today's leader needs to know the secrets that make the difference between winning and losing.

As I've gone about making a living and a life as an entrepreneur all these years—learning even more, frankly, from my mistakes than from those things I did right to begin with—I've garnered some insights I believe will help you, the reader. I originally wanted to record them for my children so they could learn from my experiences and not repeat all my miscues. As I wrote, though, I came to believe these insights could be of value to a wider audience as well.

True, Sweet Success

Perhaps the most important lesson I've learned is the definition of true, sweet success. I paid a steep price for this piece of wisdom. Let me tell you the story.

At age twenty-eight, I was a typical, hard-charging entrepreneur. I was actually a schoolteacher, but I also had three businesses going on the side, all of them making money. I enjoyed a great family, including a wife who stood behind me in whatever I wanted to try next. I was coasting along, never having suffered a serious setback up to that point. As the song goes, things were looking good and only getting better.

All that changed drastically early one morning.

On our way to work that day, I was driving with two other people in my car. As we cruised down the two-lane road at sixty miles per hour, suddenly an oncoming car veered directly into our path. I had always thought I could safely steer myself out of danger in such a situation, but this happened so fast that I simply had no time to react except to stomp on the brakes.

In a heartbeat, the two vehicles plowed into each other head-on at a combined speed of about one hundred miles per hour. And in that instant, three hearts stopped beating. The two people in the oncoming car and the passenger beside me were dead.

When the police and rescue workers arrived on the scene, they checked me for a pulse and decided I was dead, too. Understandably, they moved on. But as they climbed into the back of the car to extract Hank, my surviving passenger, he urged them to check me again. "I heard him groan," he insisted.

To their surprise, I was indeed alive. They couldn't get my broken body loose from the car at first, though, as my right leg had gotten tangled up in the smashed and bent wreck of the front end. Only after a lot of twisting, turning, and pulling could they free me and put me in the ambulance.

I languished in a coma for a month. My leg had been crushed so badly that the circulation was nearly destroyed. The doctors worried about gangrene taking hold. The leg and even my life hung in the balance.

Eventually I came out of the coma, and my leg recovered. Even after being released from the hospital, though, I faced nine months in a wheelchair. At times I could barely hold my head up, and I lived in constant pain. When I started rehab, learning to walk all over again, the pain grew even worse.

It was during those nine months that I began to wonder, *What difference does having a lot of money really make?* When you're hurting, when you stop to think about what makes life worth living, when you consider what's of eternal value, money and a fancy title and material possessions fade into insignificance.

So what does matter? What's worth living for and of eternal value? Eventually I concluded that it boils down to walking with God as you rely on his promises, loving people, and doing work that you enjoy while meeting the needs of others and making their lives better.

You Can't Do It Alone

This basic understanding of true success is so important, because our core beliefs and values shape our words and actions. That is, they hold the power to set the direction for our lives.

In the process that began after my accident, I've learned that a successful leader has a "there you are" perspective rather than a "here I am" mind-set. His or her focus is on helping others, not on being catered to; on "What can I give?" not "What will I get?" In the words of Scripture, he or she seeks to serve, not to be served.

I've also learned that leaders create a spirit within their organizations by the things they say and the way they live day by day. Their example, more than any mission statement or policy manual, sets the tone for what workers accomplish and how. They determine whether employees show up only for a paycheck or because they feel respected and therefore loyal to the organization and committed to its success.

I've learned, too, that because human nature is prone to fatigue, temptations of various kinds, and the pursuit of self-aggrandizement, leaders find it nearly impossible to succeed in the true sense on their own. The good news, however, is that we don't have to do it alone. The God who made us all has said that if we will trust in him and allow his Spirit to work in and through us, he will enable us to demonstrate daily those traits that lead to true, sweet success.

In the end, this is the greatest leadership secret of all, the missing dimension in most discussions of how to succeed as a leader. As you'll see in the pages of this book, it's the solid foundation on which to build your own success. It's immensely practical, and it has been tested and proved in my life and the lives of countless others. Come with me, and let me show you just what I mean.

MAKE SURE EVERYONE'S TALKING

The finest chocolatiers stir melted chocolate as it cools to prevent "bloom," or the gray and white speckles that surface when chocolate isn't tempered properly. (When melted, the sugar crystals in chocolate separate and the cocoa butter rises to the top, unless all is stirred to reunite the crystals and create a shiny smoothness.)

In the same way, a winning leader stirs every member of his team to stay focused on a common goal, work together, and produce a pleasing result by communicating clearly and often.

We had partnered with a small European chocolate company to help it make inroads in the U.S. market. It seemed like a good match.

Our candies were hand dipped, while theirs were molded. We were an all-American company, while they had the "prestige" of being imported from the Old World, where fine chocolates were born. We were already established vendors with the better department stores, while they were the new guys on the block. Our chocolates were too expensive for midlevel department stores and grocery stores, but theirs could be a good fit in these new markets.

All things considered, we figured that this partnership would give us a great one-two punch. But things didn't work out nearly as well as we had hoped.

The store buyers proved reluctant to give this new, unfamiliar brand a try. They showed some interest, but they were inclined to give their shelf space to established companies. Our sales were disappointing, to say the least.

Now, a fairly common practice at the wholesale level is "buying" space in retail stores in order to guarantee that your product will get placement on the shelves.

Though other companies paid these slotting fees readily and considered it standard business procedure, our firm had never done it. I always figured that if you offered a good product and good service at a competitive price, stores would want to work with you. Frankly, the practice seemed a little shady to me.

With sales of the European brand lagging, however, the owner of that company proposed that we pay a top store to carry his chocolates. The hope was that this would make other grocery store owners think the brand was doing well and want to jump on the bandwagon.

All the members of my management team knew about this suggestion, and some said it could well kick-start the brand and crank up the profits for us. A potentially large sum of money was at stake; a losing effort could become a big winner. But I just couldn't get comfortable with the idea.

After a short internal discussion, we called the other company's president back and explained why we wouldn't follow that course. I spoke gently, letting him know that I understood his frustration with the lack of sales, but I also made it clear that we would not reconsider our choice. In the end, we never did make any money with that European brand.

The simple fact is, however, that I was behind the times. Slotting fees were becoming standard, not only in grocery stores, but in many other kinds of retail businesses as well. And the other simple fact is that effective communication did not take place between me and my sales and marketing managers. They knew that slotting fees were by then normal and ethical, but I refused to accept the message, leaving me badly out of touch.

Successful leadership means, in part, making sure that everyone in the enterprise is talking about such important things as changing practices within your industry. One reason is so everyone will have a common understanding of how business is done and why. Then, when crucial decisions need to be made in crunch time, the whole team is on the same page. When that's not the case, you can lose great opportunities.

It's easy to assume that clear, effective communication is taking place between . . .

- A supervisor and the staff members who report to him or her
- "Frontline" workers and support people (e.g., accounting and computer services)
- Departments, such as manufacturing and sales, that need to work closely together if they're to be successful in their jobs
- The organization and its best, core customers

Unfortunately, the reality of the situation is often far removed from this ideal. And when everyone isn't talking clearly and being understood, the results can only be less than desirable. That's why a successful leader has to constantly make sure effective communication is taking place.

Let me suggest six specific areas in which a leader does well to focus attention on his company's communications, and let me assure you that these are lessons I've often had to learn in the school of hard knocks.

Each is a step that puts you more firmly on the path to success.

Communications Checkup

1. Value Your Values

Whether or not we think much about them, all individuals and all organizations have core values. These are beliefs about what's good and bad, right and wrong, important and inconsequential, worth pursuing and not worth the time and effort. These values guide what we think and feel, what we say, and how we act.

These values matter. They have major consequences. And employees are acutely aware of whether their leaders act in a manner consistent with the company's stated values. Whenever it would be expedient to set aside those values—it would make a situation easier or it would save money, for instance—a leader is "on trial" in the eyes of his or her staff.

This is why a leader does well to think long and hard about the values for which he's willing to take a stand and by which he's ready to be judged. Then, in written policy statements, in speeches to staff, in corporate newsletters, in meetings, and even in lunchroom conversations, he communicates those values to one and all. He invites questions, and he explains and clarifies as often as needed. Then he makes sure his actions match his words.

I recommend the following as values that a leader might want to consider embracing and communicating:

- Put people ahead of product or profit.
- Value integrity more than profit.

- Know that the company exists to meet the needs of its customers with products and/or services.
- In business as in life, treat others the way you want to be treated.
- Tell the truth, even when it hurts.

These values and others worth pursuing appear in the pages of Scripture.

2. Respect Your Staff

One of the good values I just recommended was putting people ahead of product or profit, and communicating respect for staff is a key part of that. (This also will inspire them to respect one another.) Without your people following you willingly, you're no leader at all. How you speak to them and treat them every day, in every interaction, builds a relationship that will make or break you and your enterprise.

As leaders, we typically have more on our plates than we can accomplish. Making time to talk with staff members and getting to know them may fall pretty low on the priority list. And even if we're willing to make the time, we'd better approach the relationship with gentleness, which includes humility, if we expect any real communication to take place.

Gentleness doesn't come naturally to most people, especially to those of us who tend to end up in leadership positions. You are more likely to hear *harsh* and *hard-nosed* if you ask people to describe their bosses. So from where will this gentleness that I'm advocating come? It grows out of living in close, daily relationship with God's Spirit, allowing him to work in and through us. It's part of the fruit he produces in such a life.

Let me give you an example of how gentleness in talking with staff made a major impact in my chocolate company.

At one point, we in senior management realized that we needed to know our crew in the factory better, so we made sure to eat lunch one day a week in the employee break room. We sat at a table full of people and joined in the conversation.

In doing this, we were privileged to meet an employee named Carlos, who didn't say much. Curious, we sat with him several times in the following weeks and began to sound him out.

To our amazement, as we asked Carlos about his work and how the shop was run, we discovered that he had great ideas for making things run better. *This guy has real leadership potential,* I told myself after one of our early conversations. Because he had limited English skills, however, his potential had gone unrecognized and untapped.

Carlos knew that his poor command of English would always be an obstacle to companywide leadership. In talking with our human resources people, though, we thought he might give good direction to a small department where he was also involved in the hands-on operation. We decided to try him out as manager of the kitchen.

Well, Carlos simply thrived in his new responsibility. His approach to planning the work and handing out assignments to his staff was excellent. Under his supervision, the kitchen became one of our smoothest running departments in the chocolate factory. And it all started because our senior staff showed a little respect and made the time and effort to get to know him.

3. Give Problem Staffers Time and Opportunity

The flip side of a situation like Carlos's, where you've got a quiet but potentially outstanding employee, is that of a troublesome worker. The temptation for a manager is to just get rid of the difficult employee and move on, because you have it in your power. But I've found that, again, taking the time to talk and understand the situation better can yield huge dividends.

Another of our workers, Bob, was a solid, dependable guy who nonetheless quickly wore out his welcome in every department to which we moved him. Curious about why he had so much difficulty getting along with coworkers, I called him into my office a few times to talk. He seemed bright enough and communicated easily, so I found myself scratching my head.

Then one day as we chatted, the answer hit me. Bob was so bright that he was yards ahead of everyone else—so much so that he quickly analyzed any new department to which he was transferred and formed ideas about how things there could run better. He also was quick to "share" his ideas with his new coworkers. His insights did not find appreciative audiences. He threatened the comfortable status quo and his supervisors' sense of security.

As an experiment, I assigned Bob to study the whole flow of product through our factory and suggest improvements. I was amazed when he soon came back with a detailed plan that would significantly enhance our operations. So then human resources and I decided to move him to a position troubleshooting the entire production process, and week after week he gave us phenomenal input.

Taking the time and effort to communicate gently had turned a troublesome employee into one of our most valuable workers.

4. Eradicate TMI

While plentiful, two-way communication is generally a good thing, there is such a thing as too much information (TMI). And when your organization falls victim to TMI, the result can be confusion rather than clarity.

How well I remember the time back in the early 1980s when we took the plunge and computerized our factory. Once we got through the transition period (which gave new meaning to the word *challenge*) and had the systems up and running, suddenly there was no end to the detailed data we could have.

Did sales want to know which day of the week was best for sales of a particular line of chocolates? In which part of the country? In what kind of packaging? In which types of stores? The permutations seemed infinite. Just put in your request to accounting (which ran the system) and you'd soon get back reams of reports.

I recall a staff meeting several weeks into this brave new world when the table was stacked high with computer printouts. The people from sales, marketing, manufacturing, and every other department all had their piles of data. We had to peek out from behind our piles to see each other!

Clearly, the situation had become ridiculous. We found ourselves so buried in interesting information that we now struggled to sort out what was truly important. We had become unwitting victims of TMI.

What all of us had to learn was the difference between "good to know" and "need to know." We could spend hours trying to digest stuff that was good to know but not essential to doing our jobs. It seemed like a wise use of time, but it actually kept us from completing our work.

Gradually, with experience, we learned to make that distinction between "good to know" and "need to know." The result was the elimination of about 70 percent of those interesting but voluminous reports.

5. Know Who's Who

Another key area in making sure everyone is talking is to know the personalities of the people with whom you interact regularly. Because different folks think differently, look at life differently, and work differently, working effectively with them means communicating with each person according to his or her bent.

Whole studies have been done and books written about personality types. Many psychologists and other writers, for simplicity's sake, say there are four primary types and that most people fall into one of those categories or a blend of two. For our purposes in this section, I'll make it even simpler and talk about two basic types of people: left-brained and right-brained.

The left-brained types tend to be those who have schedules and agendas that they stick to, no matter what. They're on time for every meeting, and they need to be given an assignment just once and can then be depended upon to complete it on budget, on strategy, and on time.

The right-brained people are what I call, in general, the creative types. They bring color, fresh perspectives, and unique solutions to an organization. They're the exclamation point to everything you do! They can also drive you crazy unless you accept the fact that they're different and learn to communicate with them.

Paul, a top guy in our company, was right-brained. One of the most creative people I've known, with innovative approaches to just about every aspect of his job, he was a tremendous asset to our firm. He was also literally incapable, on his own, of getting any assignment done on time.

Once I realized that was Paul's nature and that he wasn't deliberately pushing my buttons as a left-brainer, I didn't hold it against him anymore. I learned to work within that framework. When we gave him a new project, I talked with him about a plan for getting it done. He wanted small deadlines and weekly—or even daily—check-ins. If his final deadline was in six weeks, we made the first small part due in one week. Then the next part was due the week following, and so on. Invariably, when I checked in with him, he was a little behind schedule, but he was developing great ideas. I told him how impressed I was and encouraged him to keep going.

Then, the day before the meeting, I called Paul one last time to see where things stood. "I'm really looking forward to your presentation," I told him. I know he was up until two or three in the morning following many of those conversations, but he showed up at the meetings with a completed, winning project in hand.

We all have a tendency to want others to be like us, to think and work the way we do. But that's not realistic, and I've come to see that it wouldn't even be good. That insight, more than any other, has helped me to become a better communicator with the members of my team.

6. Listen to Customer Feedback

Finally, another area where good communication is essential is with your customers or constituents, as the case may be. Simply put, the successful leader will demonstrate and teach respect for customers, will encourage customer feedback—especially complaints—and will listen carefully to the feedback when it comes.

At one time my son David and I owned a restaurant featuring chicken-fried steak, a popular dish in Fort Worth, Texas. We offered a quality product, dipping each cutlet by hand in fresh batter before frying it. When you have a full house, though, with thirteen tickets waiting for attention in the kitchen and at least one order for chicken-fried steak on each, it's easy to start panicking. When you're also short a cook, the panic becomes almost unavoidable.

As we were "chewing" on all that, a vendor showed up pushing prebreaded, frozen steaks. "Think how much time you could save," he said, "and your customers won't even know the difference."

Not being a connoisseur of chicken-fried steak, I thought his product tasted fine. David, however, thought the frozen cutlet was noticeably less tasty, and he urged me not to make the switch. After talking with the kitchen manager and looking at the cost and time factors, I overruled David's concerns and decided to try the frozen product.

Well, our core customers *were* connoisseurs of chicken-fried steak, and they immediately picked up on the change. They didn't like it, to put it mildly. I vividly recall the scene as one of them told me, while paying his bill, "I guess you're doing like the rest of them and going for money instead of quality." Ouch! And, as if that weren't bad enough, he then added, "This will be my last time here. If you're going to offer a lower-quality steak, what else will you try to get past us customers?"

At that moment, obviously, I wished I had listened to David. But I couldn't turn back the clock, so I thanked the man for his honesty and asked him to give us another chance. If he would, I told him I'd pick up the tab for his next visit (*after* we'd switched back to freshly battered meat).

I also vowed—and made it a company policy—that in the future we'd ask a few key customers to sample new products and give us their feedback before making any decisions affecting their dining experience in our restaurant.

Just think what would have happened if I hadn't been hit over the head and forced myself to listen to that irate customer! On another day I might have considered him a crank or a nuisance. I would have ignored his comments and continued to use the frozen product because it was cheaper and more convenient, and I would have learned nothing from the exchange. And I would have instilled that attitude in my employees. In that case, though, everyone would come out a loser.

Make the time to talk with staff and customers—gently, so they'll be candid. (It takes a lot of gentleness to coax a customer to tell you what you're doing wrong, which is what you really need to know.) Listen to what they have to say. Check on whether people within the organization are talking with one another and with customers, rather than just assuming it's happening. This aspect of leadership won't show up on any project report, yet few things equal its importance to success.

Can You Taste Success?

1. What systems do you have in place for making sure good communication is taking place within your organization? Are you just assuming that it's happening?
2. Do those who work with you understand and share your core values? How do you know?
3. The last time you had a problem with a staff person, how did you handle it? How might you have handled it differently based on what you've read in this chapter?
4. Spend a half hour skimming through the current reading stack in your office. How much of it is truly "need to know" versus just "good to know"? What changes in handling this material could make you more productive?
5. What mechanisms do you have for encouraging and processing customer feedback? What changes might be needed in this area?

LEAD RATHER THAN MANAGE

Some chocolate makers are so focused on managing costs that they miss what brings in customers to begin with: extraordinary delicacies made from superior ingredients. Is a fine chocolate really so fine (or even chocolate), after all, if made from carob or artificial chocolate?

Winning leaders know the priorities of their organization or business enough to guard exactly which costs, ideas, people, and resources are priceless.

At one point, we saw a real need to upgrade our efficiency in purchasing supplies for our factory. We were buying too much of some supplies, which then sat in a storeroom for weeks. Other things we needed—chocolate-making ingredients or shipping materials—we ran out of before the next deliveries came, causing us to lose time until we had restocked.

An experienced purchasing agent named Roberta seemed to be just what the doctor ordered. She joined our team with great ideas for new procedures and computerized monitoring of our supplies, which would help us to set up what's now called "just in time" inventory control. She really had a knack for it, even building in extra time for deliveries from northern parts of the country in winter.

Under her supervision, stocking went even better than we had hoped. We couldn't have been more pleased.

Then one day, as I walked by Roberta's office, I saw a vendor sitting outside, waiting to see her. "Do you have an appointment?" I asked.

"Yes," he answered.

"For what time?" I said.

"Three o'clock."

I looked at my watch and saw that it was 3:30.

I let it pass at the time but later mentioned the incident to Roberta, reminding her that we had a corporate value of respecting everyone, including vendors. Our policy stated that we keep no one waiting for an appointment.

Roberta explained that she had been on the phone with another vendor at the time and was running a little late that day. So I dropped the matter and forgot about it.

A few days later, however, I again saw a vendor sitting outside her office who—when I asked about it—said he'd been waiting more than half an hour.

It disturbed me to see this taking place again, so I told Roberta not to let it happen anymore. She said she'd be more careful in scheduling appointments.

Unfortunately, as a little more time went by, the problem persisted. We heard later that Roberta told another employee that having people waiting for her made her feel important. And no matter how much the human resources people and I talked with her, she just couldn't get this area of her job under control.

In the end, my senior staff and I decided that we had to let her go. Though she was performing some aspects of her job well, if we couldn't trust her to uphold this company value, we'd have trouble trusting her in general and delegating other responsibilities to her.

Someone with what I call a "managerial mind-set"—focusing only on accomplishing the immediate job at hand—might have looked solely at how Roberta was doing with the nuts and bolts of her job, ignoring other issues. A leader, however, has to consider the big picture.

A managerial mind-set person might have let things go for a while, hoping that Roberta would come around eventually and make a confrontation unnecessary. A true leader tackles problems promptly.

It is deceptively easy. Any leader with more than one person to supervise can get bogged down in a million daily details of the work. Any leader with even a bit of insecurity or perfectionism can refuse to delegate, adding to his or her own burden and frustrating the team. Any burdened leader can neglect to read and research to stay ahead of the pack, sooner or later losing sight of where the organization ought to be going.

A successful leader will recognize these dangers and learn to lead rather than get trapped in a managerial mind-set, to focus more on doing the right things than on just doing things right, "by the book."

These and the traits I mentioned in the opening story are some of the qualities that distinguish true leaders from those who merely manage. And success stems from becoming a true leader. In my experience, it's when we're pursuing leadership at this level that God's Spirit also fills us with joy in the task, because we're seeking to make the most of every opportunity he provides.

Altogether, I've observed seven key characteristics of such people.

True Leaders versus Mere Managers

1. Leaders Go Home for Dinner

Everyone connected in any way to an organization (or any part of it) has ideas about how things ought to be done and how the leader should do his or her job. It is literally impossible to please all of them, and it's a bad idea even to try. Yet that's exactly what many leaders do.

It's a strong temptation, and I've struggled with it constantly myself. But one resolution has helped me keep a healthy perspective over the years. Early on, as I considered how to conduct my life and my business in ways that would please God, I came to the conclusion that my wife and kids had to remain my first priority. I'd heard already of too many people who had tried to build their companies by working sixteen to eighteen hours a day, allowing their families to erode in the process.

I didn't want that to happen to my family. So I decided that I was going to be home for dinner every night with my beautiful wife and three children.

Now, that might not sound like a big deal, but when you're the boss—and even when you encourage all your staff to make family a priority—the workaholics on your staff are going to expect you to be the last one out the door every day. (I guess it's kind of like expecting the captain to be the last person to leave a sinking ship!) As I left the office each evening, I could feel the quizzical looks being exchanged behind my back. And as the company grew, the pressure to work into the night grew as well.

If I'd stayed later, I could have considered more deals. If I'd put in more hours, I could have given personal attention to more details of the business. But I wouldn't trade any of those "opportunities" for the sense of rightness I felt when I heard my wife say to our kids, with pride in her voice, "*Your* daddy comes home every night for dinner."

I'm convinced, too, that looking after my family that way and knowing that all was well on the home front helped me to be more effective in leading my company than if I'd spent extra hours in the office.

2. Leaders Do More Than Oversee: They Inspire

A wise man once wrote, "Where there is no vision, the people perish" (Prov. 29:18 KJV). Truer words were never penned. And it falls to a true leader to see to it that his or her people have an inspiring vision to pursue.

It's tempting to think that this need for a vision, or a sense of mission, applies only to those doing humanitarian or religious work, or maybe to military troops who prepare to defend freedom against evil forces in the world. But the fact is that no matter what kind of work our enterprises do, our people need a vision.

An automaker might have a vision for building safe, reliable, stylish cars.

An insurance company's mission might be to provide security, service, and peace of mind to policyholders.

A janitorial services firm might have a vision for providing a clean, safe, pleasant working environment for its clients.

A grocery store's mission might be to offer a wide variety of fresh, nutritious foods at fair prices to its customers, in a convenient location.

And a maker of fine chocolates could have a vision for providing its customers fresh, high-quality candies that turn an ordinary day into a special occasion.

It's only natural, though, that people in any line of work get caught up in the day-to-day routine: meetings, deadlines, red tape, frustrations, the nine-to-five grind. And when they do, they easily lose sight of whatever sense of mission they might have had.

People with managerial mind-sets, their own noses firmly pressed to the grindstone, have no more vision than those they supervise. Leaders recognize how crucial vision is and make the time and effort to keep casting a vision for those who follow—a vision that inspires, that gives meaning to the work, that instills pride, and that motivates people to keep giving their best effort to the cause.

3. Leaders Give Their People the Power to Succeed

As I mentioned at the beginning of this chapter, any leader who is the least bit insecure will find it difficult, if not impossible, to delegate work to subordinates. The same is true of a perfectionistic leader who thinks there's only one right way to do any job: exactly the way he would do it.

Such a leader gives out assignments, but then he wants to micromanage the work. Either he's constantly looking over the shoulders of his staff, driving them crazy, or he's giving them the responsibility but not the authority to get things done, forcing them to come back to him for approval at every stage and for every decision.

And all the while this "leader" is hovering over his staffers, he is neglecting his own work, the tasks waiting on his desk that ought to be his top priorities.

A true leader, on the other hand, hires good, competent people, makes sure they have the necessary training, and then gives them both the responsibility for a job and the authority to make things happen. One of his rewards is then the joy of watching them grow and succeed.

My wife, Judie, is an entrepreneur in her own right, running her own successful cooking school. Like many, she has struggled with delegation, knowing that the school's reputation is on the line in every program, every class. A fairly recent experience, however, helped her to make great progress in this area.

She had an idea for a new program that would show parents the pleasures and the how-to's of cooking with their kids. The idea had great potential. It seemed that almost every parent to whom she mentioned it responded with an enthusiastic "When can we sign up?" The only problem was that she was already so busy running her existing programs, she simply had no time to plan and develop this new class.

What to do? To her credit, she realized the idea would never get off the ground if she tried to do it herself; she needed to let someone else make it happen. So she started looking for the right people, and before too long, she found them. One had run a citywide festival thousands had attended; she obviously knew how to set plans and guide them to fruition. The other had been Judie's personal assistant, who had shown a similar knack for finding ways to get even the toughest jobs done.

Judie described her vision for the program to the two women, gave them her notes and a few words of advice, and said, "Call me if you need me." Then off they went to implement the vision.

Soon the new class was ready to go, the publicity work was done, and parents were signing up by the score. The program didn't turn out exactly the way Judie would have done it—but she'll tell you it's even better than what she had envisioned! And today she's a joyful leader, the two women have a well-deserved sense of accomplishment, and lots of parents are having fun in the kitchen with their kids.

4. Leaders Spread Out the Kudos

To the typical, hard-driving leader, cheerleading may seem to merit a low priority, or even to be a total waste of time. "They're getting a paycheck! What other motivation do they need?" I've actually heard people say that. And I've seen the grim faces and uninspired efforts of their employees.

The true leader, however, knows that people come to work with their minds and hearts full of concerns and burdens. And while cheerleading won't solve problems either at home or on the job, it will certainly lighten the load, build a sense of loyalty and camaraderie, and make the work go more smoothly.

Thus, while it may not seem urgent or productive, taking the time and effort to encourage staff is one of the most valuable things a leader can do. It starts with putting on a positive face and attitude yourself, conveying a sense of joy and "glad to be here" to everyone you meet. There is plenty of pain and heartache in the world, and work is work, but why not be a beacon of positive energy and hope for those whose paths you cross?

Encouraging staff also means writing notes of thanks and appreciation. It means giving kudos publicly at every opportunity—for extra effort, for good ideas, for finding ways to cut costs or to provide better service to customers, and so on. It means being generous with handshakes and pats on the back (both verbal and physical). It means making the workplace fun by holding contests, sharing laughs in the break room, and having potluck lunches and company picnics. And it means getting to know your staff well enough that you learn what lifts the spirits of each.

I remember bringing donuts to a meeting of my senior team one time, and one of the guys really loved the chocolate cake variety. After that, I always tried to remember to have those for him whenever I brought pastries.

One of our top managers loved to eat popcorn in the afternoon. (Working around sweets all day, you can really start craving salt.) This was back in the days before microwave ovens became common. To express appreciation to her, as well as to the rest of the staff, we bought a microwave oven for the lunchroom, and she was thrilled.

At one of the first fancy food shows we attended in New York, our top marketing and sales people did a great job. By the end, we were all exhausted. So afterward we treated everyone to dinner at a fancy restaurant and then took them on the ferry out to the Statue of Liberty and Staten Island. For folks who had never visited the Big Apple before (some had never been outside Texas!), it was a day to remember.

5. Leaders Are Proactive about Problems

There's a natural human tendency to try to avoid unpleasant discussions and confrontation. Just dealing with things that aren't right in the workplace is a hassle. So even good leaders will sometimes let things slide for a while in the hope that problems will resolve themselves without intervention.

The fact is, however, that problems don't magically disappear. And in most cases, the longer a situation goes unresolved, the more it costs the organization in terms of money and/or morale.

In a manufacturing business such as making fine chocolates, we operate on thin margins. It's vital that we control costs tightly and save expense wherever we can without compromising the quality of our product. Well, one day it came to my attention that folks weren't following proper procedure in our shipping department, adding to our costs unnecessarily.

Containers get treated pretty roughly in the shipping process, so we packed our products carefully in protective cardboard boxes. Those boxes aren't terribly expensive, but when you use a lot of them, as we did, the cost adds up. So for smaller orders, we had half-size containers that cost about half the price of full-size containers.

Our shipping department, however, wasn't using those smaller boxes. Even orders that didn't fill half a full-size box were going out in the bigger cartons, stuffed with Styrofoam peanuts. Why? When it came to loading the trucks and keeping track of how many boxes were in a given shipment, the crew simply found it easier to work with boxes that were all the same size.

Now, again, each of those boxes was relatively inexpensive. Some managers would have ignored the situation, figuring there were bigger fish to fry. But when you're using thousands of them a year, the extra amount grows into a significant number. And when the whole firm is pinching pennies to squeeze out the best

44

profit margin possible, a more proactive approach is necessary.

As soon as I was sure I had my facts straight, I talked with the manager of the shipping department. She agreed that her crew had fallen into a habit of convenience, and she took responsibility for straightening out the situation. In no time at all, they were back on track.

Tackling problems head-on and right away isn't fun. True leaders accept the fact that it comes with the territory.

6. Leaders Manage More Than Minutiae

I referred at the start of this chapter to how easy it is to get bogged down in the daily details of running an organization. And the bigger the enterprise gets, the more details there will be, all screaming for attention. But people who let those details dictate their schedules and fill their working hours aren't leaders at all; they're managers of minutiae.

True leaders recognize the need to carve out time regularly for thinking, reading, and planning. For pondering the "big picture." For researching trends that will affect their organizations and considering what steps they can take, beginning now, to benefit from them—as opposed to ignorantly doing nothing and perhaps being hurt by those trends.

As you saw in the last chapter, this is another lesson I learned the hard way. I had not kept up with current business practice in terms of how businesses get shelf space for their products in retail stores, so I made a decision that cost us a partnership and potentially some big profits. Had I been reading and talking with others outside our company (and even within it), I likely would have had a much different perspective.

Since that time, I've made it a practice to block out several hours every week to research such issues as consumer trends, the latest in marketing practices, and new manufacturing methods. These things and their implications for our firm then become topics of discussion with my senior team. Leaders keep details from derailing them from this important priority.

7. *Leaders Learn*

Implicit in this emphasis is the need to listen. It's easy to jump to conclusions based on scant evidence, and it's easy to think we know it all. But if we want to understand what's going on inside our own organizations, we have to ask lots of questions of lots of people and then listen carefully to the answers. If anything's not clear, we need to ask follow-up questions and/or restate what we think we heard and ask, "Have I understood you correctly?"

Really listening—as opposed to letting your mind wander, half-listening while you consider what you're going to say next, or cutting off the speaker—requires a certain degree of humility. It implies that the other person knows something you don't but need to, that the other person has something worth your while to hear.

So-called leaders aren't big on humility. True leaders are the first to admit that they don't know everything and that they need help. I've struggled with this and continue to do so. But when I really listen, I experience the simple joy of learning something I didn't know before, and it's usually something that will indeed help me to lead my team better.

Those with the managerial mind-set are frustrated. They scratch and claw just to get through each day. They don't look forward to coming to work in the morning, and they can't wait to go home at the end of the day.

The people under them feel and act exactly the same.

Successful leaders, on the other hand, are aware of the challenges, but they keep the mission in view, and it gives them reason to forge ahead. They know whose approval matters most, and they share the load with good people. They're positive, proactive, joyful, and forward thinking.

The people under them feel and act exactly the same.

Can You Taste Success?

1. Whose approval are you seeking as you make decisions? Do you feel good about that, or might you want to consider some changes?

2. State your organization's vision in one sentence. Would those who work for you state it in the same way?

3. Think through the daily tasks and the projects you're currently handling. Which of those might you be able to delegate to others?

4. Based on your words and attitude in a typical day, would your staff say you're glad to be there or

you wish you were somewhere else? How do you know?

5. Is there some problem in your workplace that needs to be addressed? If so, how can you be pro-active in tackling it?

PROVEN HABIT 3

KEEP EVERYONE ON THE SAME PATH

Hand-dipping chocolatiers must know just how much cream center to pinch off and how much chocolate coating to apply in order to fit each chocolate into the company package.

In the same way that a chocolate factory depends on its team to agree piece by piece and person by person on a consistent quality, a winning leader knows that keeping the organization focused, with the same expectations, in pursuit of a common goal, results in just what the customer ordered.

At the time I'm writing this, the U.S. economy has been in a downturn for about three years, with little sign that things will improve anytime soon. Every day, it seems, brings new headlines of a now-old story: Another company is laying off tens, hundreds, or even thousands of employees (depending on its size and the quantity of its red ink).

Believe me, I understand the pressures those corporate leaders feel when sales are falling, costs are rising, and profits are disappearing. It's easy to think that the situation is largely out of your control, that you've been painted into a corner. And then it's easy to conclude that the only possible way of escape is to make a move in the one area under your direct control: to cut costs.

If you have shareholders and/or a board of directors, they will likely be shouting encouragement in your ears to slash expenses. If you hesitate, they'll soon be shouting warnings about the poor prospects for your future with the firm.

If your organization is like most, your single largest expense category is personnel and payroll. So with regrets and severance packages, you start laying off staff.

My chocolate company certainly went through its share of down times. And like all leaders in that situation, my senior staff and I tossed and turned through sleepless nights and stumbled through anxious days, searching for solutions. Cutting staff was one obvious possibility, and the temptation to do that was strong.

We made a commitment to each other, however, that layoffs would be our absolute last resort, when the only remaining alternative would be to turn out the lights and close and lock the doors for good. Before we got to that point, we would look for every other conceivable way of trimming costs and staying in business.

One of the decisions we made—a pretty bold move itself—was to cut our factory operations back from five days a week to four. That way we used less water, electricity, sugar, chocolate, coconut (and other fillings), paper, long-distance phone service—in short, less of everything. The savings were significant. Another benefit was that we also had fewer boxes of unsold goods stacking up in the warehouse.

Of course, working four days a week instead of five amounted to a 20 percent pay cut for everyone, which wasn't pleasant for any of us. It was, in fact, a serious hardship. But the bottom line is that we weathered the economic storms, we stayed in business, and no one lost a job because of the downturn. As soon as sales picked up again, we quickly resumed full production.

One of the key secrets to success as a leader is to keep everyone in your organization on the same path. That means shared vision. Good communication. Loyalty and mutual respect. Putting people ahead of profit (more about that in the next chapter). In a one-word summary, it means *loving* those you've been called to lead.

Now, to some hard-nosed leader types, talking about loving your staff sounds soft and sentimental. I can almost hear the groans as I sit in the study of my Fort Worth home, writing this. But I'm here to say that in my experience, nothing is more important to true and lasting success.

If a leader's actions don't back up his or her words, those who are trying to follow will first grow confused. *If we're billing ourselves as the best steak restaurant in town, why are we buying cheaper cuts of meat?* they'll wonder. *If we're advertising that we're the best tax service around, why are we being told to take shortcuts in preparing people's returns?*

Then, very soon, the confusion will turn to conclusion: *If the boss doesn't act as if he takes the mission statement seriously, I don't need to either.*

When sales are down, it's tempting to try to cut expenses in ways that compromise the mission. When the workload is heavy, or deadlines are fast approaching, it's easy to rationalize cutting corners and giving less than your best effort. Be assured, however, that your people will notice all such compromises, and they will "hear" your message loud and clear.

Be prepared, then, to back up the firm's vision statement with the way you do business day in and day out, in good times and bad.

As important as a sense of mission is, however, there's an element of leadership that's even more vital to keeping everyone on the same path.

Do More Than Hire: Love

As a leader, regardless of your level in your organization, you've got a million and one things with which to be concerned. You've got rising costs, slipping schedules, quality control issues, and contract problems, as well as reports to prepare and meetings to attend. The list goes on and on, seemingly forever. Yet if you're going to have all your staff pulling with you, nothing's more important than developing a genuine love for them and showing it in your words and deeds.

If you don't keep your focus on your people, you will find it easy to start thinking of them as numbers, as units of production, as no more than the way work gets done. Then that attitude will begin to show in your words, tone, and actions. The result will be discouraged, dispirited, and disloyal employees.

The mind-set I'm advocating is simply the well-known Golden Rule: Treat others, including your staff, the way you want to be treated yourself. That means showing respect and concern for the people, not just their productivity, and standing by them in tough times (as in the chapter-opening story)—in a word, *love*.

The flip side of the Golden Rule is that your team *will* treat you the way you treat them. If you're encouraging and respectful, they'll encourage and respect you (and everyone else in the company). If you're harsh and unreasonably demanding, they'll be short with you and others—including your customers. They will give only as much as they must to keep their jobs—until they find new positions where they feel appreciated.

Loving your staff also means being genuinely humble. Give credit where credit is due. If you and others accomplish something together, put them in the spotlight and let them enjoy the applause. If you blow it somehow—if you lose your cool, say something hurtful, or make a bad decision—admit it and apologize. It's absolutely amazing what good things these simple actions will do for your firm.

Showing love applies, too, when an employee has made a mistake. How you handle the situation will speak volumes to that person and the rest of the team. Sometimes people will do things that get you so upset, you want to spit nails. The loving response is to do what's best for the person, not what best allows you to vent your emotions.

I recall one time when we were shipping chocolates to the prestigious Saks Fifth Avenue store in New York. As a special touch for them, our distribution people were putting a round, gold label on top of the gold box; the label made the box look even bigger and shinier.

The good news is that most of the order went out in good shape. The bad news is that shortly after the order arrived at Saks, we got a call from their receiving department. Two full cases of boxes had come in with no labels attached. The Saks folks were understandably upset.

So were we. As soon as he hung up the phone, the staffer who took the call stormed into the shipping department and chewed out the person responsible for the mistake. That's what I felt like doing as well. Saks was the last customer we wanted to have forming a bad impression of our company's performance. But I had to ask myself what good that would do. The guy already knew he had blown it. The person who took the call had already shredded his ego, and that was after his own supervisor had burned his ears.

Now, I've flown off the handle more than my share of times, but on this occasion I thought things through long enough to cool down a little. In the end, I chose to bite my tongue and let the mistake pass, figuring the guy had learned his lesson without the need for any further "help" from me.

I'll also admit readily that loving my staff in the ways I've described doesn't come naturally to me. That's true for most of us. So how do we do it, day in and day out? The answer is that love is another part of the fruit of living in tune with God's Spirit. It's one of the things he motivates and empowers us to do. In the moment of decision, he can remind us and enable us to make the right choice.

Loving Is Just Plain Smart

Leaders find it tempting to think that being "tough," while unpleasant, is necessary to success—for example, cutting employees the moment red ink appears on the balance sheet. In my experience, however, loving people by showing them respect and taking care of them is the better approach, reducing expenses in the long term by reducing turnover.

Demonstrating love for people develops loyalty in them, which leads them to stick with you. You thereby save the costs of finding, hiring, and training new people, which can be considerable. You also save the downturn in productivity that persists until the new people are fully trained and up to speed.

On the positive side, just a little recognition can go a long way toward building the loyalty you hope to see. At our Christmastime company party, we gave out small trophies for accomplishments over the past year. We found as many reasons to hand out trophies as we could think of: outstanding performance in chocolate dipping, box wrapping, and so on.

Well, one time a hard worker named Sally got sick for a few days. She was a line worker who had a great attitude and was extremely loyal. I decided to go by her house on my way home one night just to see how she was getting along.

Her home was quite small—maybe eight hundred square feet. As I walked into the tiny living room, I first noticed Sally in a chair, wrapped up in a blanket. Then a glint of gold caught my eye. There, in the center of her mantel, in the place of honor, sat one of those little trophies. She had received it a few years earlier, and I had long forgotten why we had given it. But that bit of recognition had clearly been and remained a big deal to her, and she had done her best to "repay" the company ever since.

Use Savvy in Placing Your Players

The manager of a baseball team needs to know his personnel and put each player in the best position to help the team win. That's a key part of how he gets everyone pulling together toward the "mission" of winning games and championships.

The guy who's quick and has good hands and a strong arm probably belongs at shortstop. The guy with the strongest arm should probably be a pitcher or, if he's a good hitter, maybe the right fielder. The big, powerful guy who can't cover much ground may fit best at first base, and so on.

In the same way, as a leader in your organization, you'll have people pulling together better if they're in the positions best suited to their talents and temperaments. That means knowing your "players" and making sure their jobs are good fits for them and for your team as a whole.

We had a sales vice president in our chocolate company who excelled at calling on large accounts. He did his homework beforehand and was more than prepared to address any questions or concerns they had. And he knew how to close the deal, not being shy about asking for the big order. Not only was he extremely good with these accounts, but he was our only salesperson who felt comfortable working with them.

Problem was, the vice president spent much of his time handling the everyday questions and problems of his sales staff. As their boss, he had to try to find satisfaction in helping them succeed. He did his best to fit into the role, but we could tell he was always chomping at the bit to get into the field himself with those big accounts.

In short, we had a talented guy in the wrong position.

To make the best use of his abilities, and to help the whole team function more smoothly, we brought in another manager to assist the field salespeople with their daily issues. He found the role challenging and satisfying, and he excelled in it. And that freed the vice president to spend the majority of his time pursuing those large accounts, where he found satisfaction.

If we use the baseball analogy, that vice president had been such a good pitcher that we had promoted him to a coaching position, where his job was to train and supervise other pitchers. But he still had the talent and the heart of an ace starter, and he wanted to be on the mound, not on the bench! When we got him and the other sales manager into the right slots, both thrived, as did our sales.

How You Speak Is as Important as What You Say

Good communication is obviously important to keeping everyone on the same path. That's a subject I'll return to throughout this book. But at this point, let me emphasize the need for a leader to watch his or her words carefully. If you say the wrong thing, or even something relatively innocuous but with a certain tone, it can convey an unintended message and send people off in a wayward direction.

Here's an example of what can happen. In one of the restaurants I owned, we were making and serving our own warm, soft bread. The taste was wonderful, and customers often complimented us on it and said it was a major reason they returned to dine with us. As it sits waiting to be served, however, fresh bread has a tendency to dry out a little and get crisp.

One day in a team meeting, I mentioned that fact and explained that a customer had recently complained about his bread not being as good as on previous occasions. So I said the wait staff should make sure the bread was soft before serving it. Simple, right? No big deal, no change in policy; just a reminder of one of the "little things" you want to make sure is right for your customers.

Well, one evening shortly after that meeting, I overheard a customer objecting as he left after his meal that he hadn't been served any bread. I discovered who his waitress had been, found her, and asked why she hadn't given the customer bread.

"There wasn't any soft bread at the time," she answered confidently. "You said the other day not to serve bread if it wasn't soft."

That wasn't quite what I had said, of course, and it certainly wasn't what I had meant. Bread that had been sitting out for a while could be warmed up again, which restored some of the softness. My caution had been to make sure the bread was tasty, not to deny it to customers if it wasn't perfect.

As I reflected on the incident later that night, I realized that sometimes when I get upset, my tone can become a little stern and demanding. Since I had been talking in that meeting about a customer complaint, I had probably come across that way. And so the waitress had interpreted my simple comment as a complete change in our bread policy.

Clearly, that kind of misunderstanding can happen easily and without your even being aware of it at the time. So watch your words—and the way you say them.

Check in Regularly

To keep everyone on the same path, feeling respected and appreciated and loyal, you also need to listen to your staff. And you need to do it intentionally and regularly.

We always expected the managers in our chocolate company to listen to employee concerns. But one night, as my family talked shop at the dinner table, my daughter, Teresa, made the practical suggestion that we should have the managers allot time specifically for that on a regular basis. That made sense to my senior staff when we discussed it soon after, so we granted each manager one hour every other week for that purpose.

We encouraged the managers to set aside rank for that hour and invite their people to say whatever was on their minds. We recommended they ask things such as "What can we do to make your job go better?" "What tools do you need?" "What information do you need?"

When everyone saw that we were serious, and that we took action on their concerns and suggestions when appropriate, they knew we cared and their opinions mattered to the management. The spirit of the place, and the sense of unity, moved up a very noticeable notch or two.

Don't Take Good Times for Granted

Finally, if you're going to keep everyone on the same path and the same page, you have to stay involved. It's tempting to think that when you've established a clear vision for the organization, you've got a good team and effective systems in place, and everything seems to be running smoothly, you can relax. You can go play golf every afternoon if you want, or you can stay in your office all day and read a magazine.

It doesn't work that way. As the leader, you need to be there to show the staff that you enjoy coming in to work as much as you hope they do. You need to walk around, talk with them, praise their efforts, and listen to their concerns.

Picture Steve Martin in the popular film *Father of the Bride*. His character, George Banks, owns an athletic shoe company, and in all the scenes where you see him at work, he's walking the factory floor. He addresses individual workers by name, and he asks detailed questions about their families. Clearly, he knows them and their situations, and he has great respect for them. He cares about them as people and as coworkers.

This aspect of leadership was a challenge for me, especially in the early years. I wanted to stay up in the executive area and look at the big picture, make plans, crunch the numbers, and work out companywide problems. Walking the floor, getting to know the people, and listening to their needs and wants did not fit my agenda.

As I've said throughout this chapter, however, I've come to see that showing love for your staff by caring for and respecting them is about the most important part of a leader's job. It's also good business. And it's the foundation for keeping everyone working together toward a common vision.

Can You Taste Success?

1. Based on what you've read in this chapter, how well would you say you love your staff?
2. One definition of love is that you put the interests of the other person ahead of your own. How might you love your employees better in this regard?
3. Thinking of your staff as a team, consider this: Are all your players in the right positions? How do you know? What repositioning might be worth trying?
4. How could you do a better job of listening to your staff?
5. What changes can you make in the next week or two to get or stay more involved with your team?

PUT GOOD WORK AHEAD OF MONEY

Even though a machine can crank out ten times as many finished chocolates in a given time as a hand-dipping line, a premium chocolate factory can ensure a better candy with more attentive work: a softer and smoother center, a more attractive appearance, and a superior taste.

Likewise, the winning leader defines good work, is committed to it, and sees how profits result because of—and not in spite of—it.

very business has to make a profit. Even nonprofits have to take in more than they spend or the boat just won't float. The purpose of a business, however, is to provide good products and services to customers; profits are normally the result of doing that well. Forgetting that, and putting profit at the top of your priority list, can sometimes lead to disaster.

For a while, I had a senior staffer named Pete who was a genius at making money, squeezing the most out of every dime. I marveled at some of his techniques. Because he was so good at finding every feasible way to turn a profit and his focus was on making the numbers for every quarter look as positive as possible, his thinking often greatly influenced my own.

This usually had beneficial consequences, but once it almost caused us a lot of pain, frustration, and, ultimately, money as well.

Our chocolate factory had been in the same location for many years, but business was strong and growing. We found ourselves in the pleasant dilemma of needing more space so we could increase output to meet demand, but we had no room to expand. Our twenty-thousand-square-foot facility was holding us back. What were we to do?

Demand was growing steadily. In addition, several potentially big deals were in the works. I suggested that we be forward thinking and find a facility that would not only meet our immediate need for more space, but also enable us to keep an unbroken supply of the highest-quality products going to our customers into the foreseeable future. Specifically, though it seemed almost incomprehensible, I proposed that we try to roughly triple our space and find a facility with at least sixty-five thousand square feet.

Pete, with his eye firmly fixed on the bottom line, argued that that was far more space than we needed. We could save a lot of money and still meet our current and near-term demand by doubling our square footage. That was a more-than-bold-enough move as far as he was concerned, and the difference in costs and in debt on the books would make the next quarterly statement look a lot better.

Our senior staff went back and forth on this. If profit in the short term had been my top priority, I eventually would have given in to Pete's logical and forceful arguments. He made a lot of sense, others on the team agreed with him, and his approach was far less risky.

However, I believed that in fairness to our employees, who would bear the brunt of the burden in making the move work, we had to look further into the future. Also, believing that our business was on the right track and would continue to grow, I didn't want us to find ourselves in a place where just a few years down the road we would be unable to keep our customers happily supplied with timely deliveries because we had again run out of manufacturing capacity!

When my view finally won over the team, we looked for and finally found a space suitable for our operations with a bit more than sixty-five thousand square feet. We bit the bullet, signed the papers, and made the move.

I'm happy to say that it proved to be one of the best moves our business ever made. Within two years, we started to expand into all areas of the new facility. If we had instead opted to save money and settle for a plant of only thirty-five thousand square feet, we would have maxed out every square inch within four years and been forced to move again—at double the cost of what we paid for our larger building.

In this case, putting good work (for our staff and our customers) ahead of profit was not only the right thing to do, but it also meant more profit in the long run.

In business, income and profit are how you keep score. When a company is publicly owned, shareholders and the investment community scrutinize every quarterly statement and penalize failure to meet expectations. Private investors like to look over management's shoulders to see how their money is being spent. The budgets of nonprofits get put under a microscope as well.

These kinds of pressures can easily and understandably cause a leader to focus on money issues—how much the organization has, how to get more and spend less, how to cut corners to boost per-unit profits, and so on. But as that opening story illustrates, while it's obvious that you have to make a profit in order to stay in business, a myopic concentration on the bottom line can prove shortsighted and even destructive to the enterprise.

An organization exists to meet the needs or wants of customers by providing quality products and services. Keeping the focus there as a leader is vital to success. This is another area, which the Bible calls *goodness*, where God's Spirit wants to help us if we'll listen to his prompting and seek his strength.

In my years of running a high-end chocolate company and other businesses, I've found that leaders need to pay careful attention to putting good work ahead of money in five particular areas.

Five Ways to Honor Work over Money

1. Never Neglect Your Core

Customers are the life's blood of any company. Taking good care of them is essential. Those facts are so obvious that it almost seems silly to write them. Yet over and over, we hear about and experience personally the terrible treatment of customers, from ignoring them to taking them for granted to acting downright rude. How many times have you visited or called a place of business, only to be treated by the staff as if you were a nuisance?

Taking care of customers can take many different forms, and whole books have been devoted to this topic. But let me give you a couple of examples of how we tried to do it in my chocolate business.

High heat greatly (adversely) affects quality chocolates, of course. Even if they don't get as far as melting completely, they can lose shape, become discolored (or "bloom," as we say in the business), and so on. So, making them in Texas, we had to ship them in refrigerated trucks for at least half the year. In the winter months, though, the need for refrigeration was marginal. We stood a good chance of getting product to our customers without heat damage in regular trucks, at a significantly reduced cost.

Since shipping was such a major expense, and the odds of getting the product delivered in good shape were high, the temptation was strong to go with the non-cooled trucks whenever it seemed the weather would cooperate.

But early on, our staff decided that if we wanted to build a reputation for supplying chocolates of the highest quality, and if we wanted our customers to be more than satisfied every time they opened one of our packages, we simply couldn't take the chance. We swallowed hard and booked all our shipments on refrigerated trucking lines. It created goodwill. People felt we really cared. It was a good example of the old adage, "Put your money where your mouth is."

Another instance of the need to take care of customers arose at the time when factory outlet stores were starting to become popular. We looked at what was happening and concluded that although our primary customers were the stores that carried our chocolates, individuals in Fort Worth (where the plant was located) might like to come by and get premium chocolates at factory-direct prices.

We opened the store, and lo and behold, we were right. Local folks loved coming to the factory and buying our candy at discount prices. The business grew rapidly, the profit margins were good, and we were patting ourselves on the back for our great idea and telling each other what marketing geniuses we were.

As it turned out, there was just one problem with our brilliant idea. But it was a biggie.

People in our factory shop were buying chocolate at half the normal retail price that area department stores charged. Naturally, those retailers couldn't compete with our prices, and so our product completely stopped moving off their shelves. To say that they weren't happy—and that they let us know it—might qualify as the understatement of the year.

What were we to do? On the one hand, the retailers were our bread-and-butter customers. On the other hand, we had a new, sizable, and growing group of customers who loved coming to our factory store. Even if we reached the logical conclusion that we needed to satisfy our core (retailer) customers, might there be some way, somehow, to please both groups?

After a brief discussion, we realized our core customers had to come first. We couldn't continue to alienate our retailer base. The factory store would have to adapt or close.

Fortunately, we hit upon the idea of selling only seconds in the factory shop—candy that was slightly misshapen or discolored, had broken corners, or had just sat in inventory too long and wasn't the freshest anymore. We could deeply discount these chocolates. The individual customers thought that was great, the retailers were pleased that we were no longer undercutting them on the top-quality candies, and we got to keep our profitable little sideline business.

2. Apply the Golden Rule to Competitors, Too

When you're going tooth and nail against a tough competitor, especially one who's given you reason to dislike him, the temptation is strong to try to increase your

70

market share by bad-mouthing him to customers. But you'll come out ahead—in peace of mind, and maybe even in profits—if you resist the temptation and refuse to talk him down.

This is yet another lesson I had to learn the hard way.

I have mentioned that at one time we had opened a home-style restaurant featuring chicken-fried steak on one of Fort Worth's main streets. We offered good food and good service and started to build the business.

Then, just five months after our grand opening, a new home-style restaurant featuring chicken-fried steak made its debut less than a mile away from us! Talk about a blow! To make matters worse, when I went in to check out the competition, I recognized the owners as guys who had taken notes while dining in our restaurant a few months before, and they were copying some of our ideas and methods. To cap it all off, I heard a short time later that these competitors were not saying the kindest things about our restaurant.

I felt I had plenty of reason to return the favor, not the least of which was that the survival of our restaurant was on the line. I was soon complaining incessantly about the other guys and what they were doing to our cash flow.

One Sunday evening, as I was ranting again about what the competition was doing to us, my daughter, Teresa, said, "This is not the dad I'm used to."

"What do you mean?" I asked. I'll never forget her answer.

"All you talk about these days is money. All you're concerned about is what they're doing to you. That's not the way you raised us kids! Where's your will to find another way and not let the money issues drive you?"

She was right. The truth of what she said hit me like a hammer, and I had no reply. But I decided then and there that though I still wasn't happy about the situation, attitudes needed to change, starting with mine.

At our next restaurant staff meeting, I told the crew, "Look, we're the originals, and we still hand-dip our steaks in fresh batter, so we know we've got better food. So from now on, if customers ask about the other guys, just say, 'Yes, they're our competitors, and we'll leave it to you to judge which place is better.'"

Taking that approach was tough, but it did make us work harder, stay sharper, and focus on our own product. I'd like to report that all of our customers rallied around us, but the biggest impact was in our own peace of mind. The other guys didn't go away, so our income was never what it might have been. Still, our collective outlook definitely improved, and I slept much better at night.

There's a passage in the Scriptures that says, "Do not let any unwholesome talk come out of your mouths, but only what is helpful for building others up according to their needs, that it may benefit those who listen" (Eph. 4:32). By tearing down my competition, I would not have been building up my staff or our customers.

3. Look beyond the Immediate Prize

Putting good work ahead of money can be excruciatingly hard when someone is offering you *a lot* of the green stuff. But doing good work as a leader means looking at more than just the immediate opportunity. Let me explain again with an illustration.

The chocolate business was doing pretty well, growing steadily but not spectacularly from year to year. Our expanding list of customers had a snowball effect; it gave us credibility and clout with potential new markets. That was the dynamic that led to "The Offer."

Buyers for the J. C. Penney department store chain had tried our candy at another store and really liked the look and taste of our product. "Would you be interested in exclusively supplying both bulk and boxed chocolates in our stores over a whole region of the country?" they asked. This represented a huge opportunity. It would increase our annual sales by more than a million dollars overnight, and it would also get that snowball of exposure and momentum moving even faster.

What was not to like about The Offer? This was the kind of deal that businesspeople dream about. We started compiling wish lists for how we would use the extra income.

Then we woke up to an unpleasant reality. To meet the demand of this one customer, we would need to expand the plant, bring in more equipment, and hire a bunch of new workers. In short, we would have to increase our overhead greatly, and we'd have to go deeply into debt to do it. As long as sales went well with this customer, we'd be okay. But what if our product didn't move through their stores so well or we had some kind of falling out? We'd be stuck with a lot of excess capacity and overhead, plus a debt load we'd have no way to carry. At the very least, we'd have to lay off a lot of skilled and loyal staff.

This was exactly why we'd planned never to let one customer represent more than 10 to 15 percent of our business. Agreeing to this deal would make this chain of stores about 25 percent of our business.

When we started raising this red flag in management meetings, the salespeople threw a fit! They couldn't believe we'd even consider walking away from such an opportunity. Their protests made me wonder if we were indeed crazy, yet the conviction was growing that we should not make ourselves so dependent on one customer. Good work in this case meant looking beyond the immediate profit potential to the possible long-term complications.

Eventually, painfully, and with a lot of second-guessing, we turned down The Offer. J. C. Penney quickly found another chocolate maker to supply its stores. Our salespeople alternately growled and groaned, as they should have.

Just two seasons later, however, we heard that Penney's decided to stop offering candy counter (bulk) chocolates in their shops. They sold off their remaining stock at deep discount.

By looking at the big picture and the long term instead of just the cash on the table, we had made the wise decision and probably saved our company.

4. Let Reason Rule

Another area in which it's vital to put good work ahead of money is in controlling emotions. With the responsibility and other pressures on leaders, we find it easy to be fearful, to get angry, to make (almost always bad) decisions that we base on feelings rather than reason.

Once again, I write from painful experience. I recall the season when we brought out a new line of chocolates called Fudge Love and Chocolate Truffles. We had spent a lot of time, effort, and money in developing every aspect of the line, including the beautiful gold box that held the candy and gave it great shelf appeal. We launched the line with high hopes of a strong return on our investment.

Shortly after the launch, however, we received a letter from one of our competitors saying that they had come to the market with a similar-looking gold box first, and we had better take ours off the market or they might sue.

I confess that the letter threw me into a panic. This competitor was a big company, much bigger than we were, and could cause us a lot of grief. It could also, I figured, bear the expense of a legal battle a lot easier than we could. I began to lose sleep at night as we considered how to respond.

One line of advice we received said we should ignore the letter. After all, there were already other candy lines in the market using gold boxes. Besides, you can't trademark a gold box! But the other line of thought said that even if we were within our legal rights, we could end up spending a lot of time and effort to defend those rights. That's not to mention the emotional roller coaster we would have had to ride.

To do my job properly, I needed to get my emotions in check and consider the situation calmly and logically. If we were indeed in the right, we needed to stand up for that, at least long enough to see whether the other guys were serious or bluffing, even if it meant running up some legal bills. Our credibility as a company was at stake, not to mention all the effort and money we had poured into the market launch for our new gold-boxed product line.

I'd like to tell you that I pulled myself together, found my backbone, and decided to hold my ground. I'd like to tell you that, but it wouldn't be true.

Instead, my anxieties ruled my will, and I caved. I gave the orders to come up with a new box as quickly as possible and to trash our remaining supply of the gold. The decision cost us a lot, but not as much as a lengthy legal battle would have cost, even if we eventually won.

Looking back on it, was it a good decision? Probably not. Later events made it clear that the competitor had been bluffing. But at the time, in my fear, it seemed like the only possible decision.

5. Take Care of Your Employees

Finally, putting good work ahead of money means taking care of your employees. It means respecting them as partners, as true coworkers, and treating them accordingly. It means seeing them as people and not just the way jobs get done. It means paying them fairly and offering such benefits as flextime to meet their needs. It means that even when there's a problematic situation that requires attention, the way you handle it is at least as important as the outcome.

I recall one of our hand-dippers, Sara, who was a great worker but whose negative personality and sharp tongue frustrated a lot of her coworkers. Their dislike of Sara was so strong that we had to consider whether or not to keep her on staff.

Now, I've seen instances in which management forces decided they wouldn't allow one good worker to sour the atmosphere for everyone, and they let the person go. I've also seen instances where management decided that because the troublemaker was the best worker on the floor, the other workers in the department could just swallow their frustration. We decided to try to find some way to keep this good worker *and* keep peace in the dipping room.

First, we chose to keep Sara because she was so good at her job (she could dip more than anyone and had the best work ethic), but we encouraged her to be more sensitive to the people around her. Then we met with the rest of the department, let them air their feelings, and explained our decision—we didn't just jam it down their throats. We also encouraged them not to take any of Sara's negative remarks personally.

After all that, the situation still wasn't ideal, but the atmosphere did seem somewhat more relaxed. And eventually, when Sara's supervisor noticed that Sara was good at describing how she did her work so well, he made her a trainer of new staff. Much to the surprise of some, she flourished in this bit of a spotlight. She seemed almost a natural at passing on all the tips and tricks of the trade that she had learned over the years.

Taking care of employees also requires giving them the freedom to do their jobs. Let me give you a couple of examples of what I have in mind.

Perhaps because of our Puritan work ethic, many in the American workplace expect employees to always look busy, no matter what the nature of their jobs. I noticed at one point that even members of my senior staff—including me—grabbed a pencil or picked up the phone if they saw someone approaching their offices. But to do our jobs well, we needed to spend some time just thinking, reading industry periodicals, meditating, and doing other "brain work" that may not look productive—it is part of that leading rather than managing I discussed in an earlier chapter.

Finally we instituted a policy that everyone at the senior level had to think or read for an hour a day. I *wanted* to see people pondering ideas and reading magazines. Eventually we all agreed that staring into space was a positive thing.

Giving employees freedom also means putting in the time to get to know them and to learn who works best in what kind of environment. Some need close supervision; some need more of a free rein. Some want to be told what to do step-by-step; others just need to know the goal and will then find their own ways there.

I once had a senior manager who ran most of our day-to-day operations in the factory and in the shipping room. He wanted to do things his way, which was different from mine, and at first we had some sharp disagreements. As time went by, though, I realized that he *was* getting the job done—very efficiently, actually. One day the obvious hit me between the eyes: There might be more than one way to skin this cat!

You have to give people adequate training and accountability. But if you've hired good people (and what other kind *would* you hire?), you also have to keep an open mind and trust them to do good work.

To stay in business, you have to stay in the black most of the time. But good work—good products and service—has to remain the primary objective. Sometimes that means doing things that may not help the bottom line in the short term. In the end, though, you simply can't enjoy real, lasting success without keeping the focus on doing good work.

Can You Taste Success?

1. What could your organization do to start taking better care of customers?
2. Whom do you see as your biggest competitors? What are you in the habit of saying about them to your staff? To customers?
3. Think of a time when you were tempted to get greedy in your business. What lessons can you learn from that experience?
4. What negative emotions do you struggle most to control in the workplace? Formulate a game plan for dealing with them the next time they arise.
5. In light of what you've read in this chapter, how can you take better care of your employees?

ALWAYS THINK OF THE CORE CUSTOMER

An artificial chocolate coating might be easier for a candy maker to handle because it's more tolerant of temperature changes, and it might be cheaper to produce because it uses tropical oils rather than cocoa butter. Yet chocolate lovers can quickly tell a fake from the real deal—and they won't settle for less.

The winning leader knows what core customers or clients want and need most to keep them coming back for more.

We thought we were doing a good job in our chocolate company: We offered excellent products, fair prices, and first-class service. Nonetheless, our sales were down about 3 percent from the previous year and showed no signs of picking up. What could we do to turn things around?

Our senior team got together to assess the situation and decide on a course of action. After chewing on it for a while, we concluded that we needed a new, less expensive line for the middle-income market. The wholesale price would be two dollars per pound lower than that for our premium line.

Now, in retrospect, that wasn't a bad decision. But the way we went about it wasn't wise, and the law of unintended consequences soon caused serious trouble.

The drop in sales had thrown me into a bit of a panic. Seeing this new line as our key to success, I pushed everyone to get it up and running as soon as possible. Though I don't recall telling the team to "drop everything" and concentrate on developing the new line, they picked up on my sense of urgency and made it priority number one, with everything else a distant second.

Before long, all the senior staff were consumed with plans for the new line. What types of chocolates should we include? More creams, caramels, or nougats? More nut fillings? More truffles? If so, what kinds? What should the total weight be?

The packaging people were likewise caught up. What should the box look like? Shape? Size? Color? Graphic design? Depending on the size and shape, how many boxes would fit in our standard carton?

The same thing happened in the shipping department. The supervisors quickly immersed themselves in such details as where we should store the new product to make putting up orders most efficient. Did we need to add on to the conveyor system? Would we need more order pickers and packers?

One packer told me, "Our supervisor doesn't look very closely at what we do anymore. Instead, she's always talking about how we're going to integrate the new line into our system."

That mind-set had become typical, and hearing comments like that should have set off alarm bells in my brain. But I was thinking that way myself, so my only reaction was, *Good, that's the kind of dedicated effort we need.*

Because of all this focus on the new line, however, we slowly and subtly started letting our core business rest on a back burner. We didn't process orders through the system in a timely way. Consequently, they didn't go out in our usual time frame. Some of our best customers started running out of product on the shelf before their new shipments arrived.

In other cases, shippers sent out incomplete orders. In a few instances, we lost orders completely, leading to irate phone calls. Our own supplies of candy-making ingredients and boxes grew dangerously low as we tried to make decisions regarding the new line.

In short, in our almost-frantic pursuit of this new "holy grail" that was going to "save" the company, we fell into the trap of taking our core customers for granted. To use a golfing analogy, we took our eye off the ball, looking up at where we wanted to go instead of keeping our attention on making solid contact with the ball. We let our standards slip, and our customers suffered as a result.

Through the loud chorus of complaints we received, along with some canceled orders and other expressions of displeasure, we finally got the message. But not before our reputation and our sales had suffered a good bit, too.

※

Every enterprise depends on customers of one kind or another, people who buy your goods or services in some way. And any leader with an entrepreneurial bent—certainly anyone in sales or who has other income responsibility—is naturally tempted to go after new customers rather than focusing on serving the existing accounts.

Going after the new is exciting; working with the old seems mundane.

Chasing the new is thrilling; servicing the old feels like a lot of hard work.

Grabbing a customer from a competitor gets celebrated as a victory; doing well with an existing account barely gets noticed.

And, as the opening story illustrated, developing a new product and getting it to market generates a lot of buzz, whereas improving the old usually yields only yawns.

You would think that sales folks, who "eat what they kill" (i.e., get paid at least partly on commission), would be drawn to the "easy pickings": existing, proven customers, who are often smaller accounts. But salespeople are generally highly competitive, and most are drawn to the "thrill of the hunt"—going after new and bigger accounts, even when it costs them.

We had one sales rep, Ted, who proved an exception to this rule. He gave his existing accounts top priority, developing close relationships with his buyers and earning their trust. As a result, every month he seemed to reach his sales goals faster and more easily than anyone else.

Others of our salespeople looked at Ted's numbers, shook their heads, and told the sales manager, "You know, I guess I need to spend more time with my current accounts, too." Then off they went to carry out this fresh, potentially lucrative resolve. Like a New Year's resolution, it usually lasted two weeks at most. Then they were back to chasing the new thrills, as we called them.

Don't get me wrong. You need to keep giving customers new reasons to buy from you, and you need to keep growing your business with new accounts. But it's all too easy to assume those existing, core customers will always be there—to call on the phone instead of making the effort to see the buyer face-to-face. To spend less time with the buyer when you *are* there. Eventually, to make less contact of any kind. Ultimately, to lose that once-good customer to a more-attentive competitor.

Do More, Not Less, with Existing Clients

Ironically, in light of those natural tendencies, paying attention to your core customers is actually good business—very good business—as seen in the story of Ted. You can always increase sales more easily and at lower expense by working with your existing accounts, as opposed to signing up new accounts. You'll have far less sales expense, lower shipping costs, and no additional accounts receivable for accounting to handle.

Recognizing those facts, we set up a system with our sales team to do more, not less, with our existing accounts. We instructed our people to go into their stores at least once a month and work with the owners or managers (in the case of a chain store). Our folks dusted any boxes that had been sitting a while, made sure everything was in the right place, and generally gave our product the best presentation possible.

Most of these store owners and managers worked long hours and had trouble staying on top of those little details. Consequently, they appreciated the extra help and felt real loyalty toward us. Their stores looked better, our chocolates sold better, and they ordered more from us—a classic win-win situation.

To make sure our salespeople maintained this practice, every time we had a sales meeting, we asked one of them to give an update on all of his or her accounts. This encouraged everyone to keep up his or her routine and not get lazy in serving existing customers.

Kindness for All

While plans and systems help to make sure things happen, the real key to not taking core customers for granted is to have an attitude of respect and consideration toward everyone—in a word, *kindness*.

87

A verse in Scripture says, "Do nothing out of selfish ambition or vain conceit, but in humility consider others better than yourselves" (Phil. 2:3). And that's actually good business practice. Kindness means:

- You focus on meeting a customer's needs and wants, not on twisting his arm or otherwise pressuring him to buy something he doesn't really need or desire.
- You never think of yourself as smarter or in any way superior to a customer.
- You go to a customer with the aim of serving, not of meeting a sales quota.
- You don't look down on smaller customers, working with them only until a "bigger fish" comes along.

Unkindness can happen so quickly and subtly in a setting such as a trade show. You're standing there in your booth, talking with a customer who has two stores. He's got your attention, and everything's going fine until the buyer for a fifty-store chain walks up to your booth. What do you do then?

Your tendency is to say "Excuse me" to the first buyer and abandon him for the second. Stop! That's not only unkind, but it may well also cost you the business of that first customer. Stay with the one who was already there. He has earned your loyalty.

To protect yourself from that kind of conflict, make sure you've got enough help on hand to assist that second buyer. If possible, make appointments beforehand. But whatever you do, don't disrespect that customer with the smaller account.

Showing this sort of practical kindness, like the other traits I'm advocating in this book, is difficult if not impossible on our own, especially in times of high stress. Once again, the power to do it comes from being in close relationship with God's Spirit. When we seek his involvement in our daily lives, kindness is one of the things he develops in us and shows to others through us.

Beating the Competition—Using Kindness

Speaking of times of high stress, kindness really gets put to the test when times are tough. But you can pass those tests with positive results.

I recall the time when I was out making calls with one of our top salespeople, Jerry. He had built good relationships with his customers and knew such details as how many kids each buyer had and what kind of work their spouses did. He showed a sincere kindness and compassion for them all.

Well, we walked into a drugstore, and the buyer, instead of greeting Jerry warmly, turned and walked away when he saw us enter. The two of us exchanged puzzled looks, then followed the guy as he retreated to his office at the back of the store.

When we got there, we stuck our heads in the door and Jerry asked, "How are things going?"

Looking down at his desk, the guy replied, "I'm embarrassed to tell you, Jerry, but headquarters told us to move your product to the bottom shelf and put this other brand at eye level. They want to see if it can compete with—maybe even replace—yours."

Jerry was clearly stunned by the news. He considered this guy a friend, and our chocolates had done well for his store. I would have understood if Jerry had responded like a man feeling hurt or betrayed. To his great credit, however, he kept himself under control and chose instead to show kindness.

"Don't worry about it," he said, managing a smile. "Have you got time for a Coke?"

The buyer, obviously relieved, offered a weak smile in return and answered, "Sure, why not?"

So we had our Cokes, the two of them chatting about family, Little League games, and swimming lessons, as if nothing had changed. When they were finished and Jerry and I got ready to leave, the buyer told Jerry, "Don't be concerned. I really don't think you have anything to worry about."

As we got back in our car, Jerry expressed his disappointment, but he also made a profound statement for a guy who's paid on commission: "My sales might be off for the next month or so, but we'll soon be back in the saddle with this account."

I left thinking he was right. The way the buyer had responded to Jerry's kindness told me that he respected and trusted Jerry all the more, and that he wanted to keep doing business with him.

As it turned out, Jerry's prediction was a little off. A full six months went by, during which time Jerry developed some new accounts to help make up for the loss of that one good account. But at the end of that period, the drugstore chain's company heads were ready to conclude that they still needed and wanted our brand in their stores. Jerry was, indeed, back in the saddle and saw a big boost in his sales and income.

Because Jerry hadn't felt sorry for himself but focused instead on serving and meeting the needs of his customer with kindness, they both came out ahead.

Consider Comfort Levels

Taking care of core customers also means that when you assign a new sales rep to a territory, your top criterion when deciding whom to send is to ask who will be the best fit with the existing accounts.

I mentioned in an earlier chapter that some salespeople like to work primarily with large customers, while others are intimidated by them. You don't want the latter kind of personality working in a territory made up mostly of bigger accounts.

Finding a good fit can also be a matter of geographical considerations. With our company being based in Texas, our standard practice was to hire salespeople locally and then send them out to the various territories across the country. We had a certain logic behind that, but our mediocre sales in California—which should have been a huge market for us—forced us to reconsider.

When the need arose to hire a new rep for a territory covering much of the Golden State, one of our sales management folks suggested, "Maybe it's time to hire someone local—someone who already lives there, who has contacts there, who knows the California market."

So that's what we did. We found a guy named Gary who, though new to the chocolate business, had a good track record in sales. He looked California, dressed California, thought California, and talked California. He had lived there a long time, loved the state, and was a great people person. We hired him, and he went to work.

The difference in sales was dramatic. Orders from existing accounts started to grow. New accounts were opened. Before long, and perennially thereafter, this guy was one of our top sellers nationwide. California finally became the kind of market for us that we had always known it could be. And today Gary is one of California's largest specialty foods distributors.

Every Customer—and Employee—Is Your Best

While the term *customer* naturally brings to mind those who buy our goods and services, we do well to remember that we also have other kinds of core customers.

For instance, when we want to pursue a certain market but it doesn't make financial sense to do so with staff people, we sign up a distributor to go after that business. The distributor essentially buys from us at a higher-than-normal discount and then resells to retail accounts.

Distributors usually carry several product lines in the same category. If you take them for granted and don't keep them informed and motivated, feeling like a vital part of your team, your sales with them will slip, and they'll start giving another company's product a higher priority in their sales efforts.

Kindness, not to mention self-interest, dictates that you treat them like your very best customers.

Employees are another sort of core customer whom you should never take for granted. As fellow human beings made in the image of God, they deserve to be shown love and kindness. That means putting their needs ahead of your own. This means that as a leader, you never slack off but work harder than everyone else to keep the enterprise strong and growing so that your staff can continue to enjoy good-paying jobs.

Again, from a self-interest standpoint, showing kindness to employees will also develop the loyalty and willingness to work hard that you want and need from them. Once more, this is just putting the Golden Rule into practice: Treat your staff the way you want them to treat you.

Remember Who Creates Your Paycheck

Finally, as organizations, we must never forget that it's not the company that pays our salaries, it's the customers. That alone, even if there were no other reasons for treating them well, makes them very important people!

As leaders, we need to keep that reality in sight. And we need to remind our people, at all levels, of it regularly. In our chocolate company, we made a point of stating it at least once in every meeting: "The paycheck may come from our accounting department, but the funds come from satisfied customers. So let's be thinking about how we're going to meet their needs today."

Taking good care of core customers isn't glamorous or exciting. Putting their needs ahead of our own isn't easy even in the best of times; it gets all the harder under tough circumstances. But it is the irreplaceable bedrock of every successful enterprise.

Can You Taste Success?

1. In a given quarter, what percentage of your sales and other income comes from existing customers?

What percentage from new accounts? If you don't already know, how quickly and easily can you get your hands on this information?

2. In light of what you've read in this chapter, how prone would you say your firm is to taking core customers for granted?

3. What measures can you take to help your team remember to take better care of core customers?

4. What are some practical ways you and your staff can show kindness to customers?

5. How can you show greater kindness to your employees?

DON'T TRY
TO GO IT ALONE

Premier chocolate is nearly impossible to shape from scratch. So upon special request for a beautiful chocolate swan sculpture to grace the dessert table at a wedding reception, even our best product creator needed help. We could have used a mold, but then there's a line where the two halves connect. A craft store actually contributed the best idea: painting a Styrofoam swan in chocolate, tempering the chocolate, and then brushing on a second coat. The result pleased the customer every time.

Just as that Styrofoam form supported this popular sculpture idea, the watchful, winning leader can find help from inside the organization—and the minds of customers, clients, contributors, and others.

When we were running a catering business out of our restaurant, we landed a contract to provide an on-site dinner for eight hundred people. That's obviously a big job, one that would require the help of a number of staffers. But it's still easy when you're the leader—especially if you founded and built up the business yourself—to hold a mind-set that says you know everything that needs to be done and can manage all the details.

Well, we had decided to provide baked chicken as the entrée. And in a setting like that, it's essential that all eight hundred pieces of chicken be cooked properly. You don't want anyone cutting into his or her meat and finding it undercooked; that person is likely to be very unhappy and very vocal. Recent news reports had highlighted the dangers of salmonella poisoning, so people were particularly anxious about undercooked food.

If all eight hundred chicken fillets weren't properly prepared, hot, and tasty—or if someone caught salmonella—not only might that customer never call again, but word would soon spread through the community and our reputation would take a major blow.

In other words, while this job offered us a great opportunity, it also offered the potential for great disaster if we mishandled it.

The goal was to get eight hundred chicken dinners cooked, hot, tasty, and in front of the diners at the same time. That was a lot of bird! The answer was that the convention hall where the event would be held had three large, commercial ovens. Doing the final cooking right there on-site would greatly help us.

Now, as I said, it's easy to think as the leader that you've got all the bases covered, everything under control. You're the big-picture guy! That's certainly the way I was thinking on this occasion. As the day of the dinner approached, I mentally patted myself on the back: *This could have turned out terrific or terrible. Thanks to my organization of the project and anticipating all the needs, it's going to be great!*

That's when my head cook and manager suggested, "Maybe before the night of the dinner, I should go down to the hall and check the accuracy of the temperature controls on those ovens."

Well, what can I say? The possibility that any of those ovens could be off had never occurred to me. But I was happy he was looking at the details, and what would it hurt to check? So he went on down.

You've probably already guessed what happened. He discovered that one of the ovens was a little off, not running as hot as the controls indicated. Approximately 267 chicken fillets were about to be served undercooked if the problem weren't caught. If the planning had been entirely my domain, that's exactly what would have happened.

This story illustrates the dangers of going it alone as a leader, and of thinking that way even when you're part of a team. We're kidding ourselves if we believe we can succeed as lone rangers. We'll be overworked and anxious, and we'll still overlook vital details.

In contrast, when we work in concert with good people, life doesn't have to be quite so "lonely at the top," and we can experience incredible peace of mind and heart.

Fortunately for the health of more than 250 people, I wasn't quite the one-man show I had imagined myself to be in arranging their banquet dinner. But it's all too easy for a leader who has enjoyed some success to become proud, to think he can know it all and do it all, that no one else could do what he can do.

The fact is, however, that in any enterprise, rarely is a person truly indispensable. For 99.99 percent of the leadership positions in the world, lots of people could do the job if given the chance. And for 100 percent of those positions, the people occupying them need the help of others if they are to enjoy either serenity or lasting success.

In light of those realities, two attitudes strike me as being appropriate for all leaders: First, we should be grateful, not arrogant. We've been given opportunities that others long to have. So let's be humbly thankful that we are where we are, able to do what we're doing.

Second, we should see ourselves as "just another log on the pile." Sure, what we do is important, but each of us is only one part of the organization. There's no way we could succeed alone; we need our coworkers as much as they need us.

A Lone Leader Is Never Enough

I mentioned in an earlier chapter that my wife, Judie, runs a cooking school. While it grew from her heart and soul, and she has been very hands-on with it from day one, it quickly became more than she could possibly handle on her own. As with all thriving enterprises, no one individual can manage all the details.

Whatever the nature of our organizations, we always want to provide a top-quality product or service to our customers. In Judie's case, her goal is always to exceed her clients' expectations. While providing cooking classes may sound simple to some, she actually has a list of dozens of details to attend to before every session: The menu has to be planned, a grocery list prepared, and the supplies purchased (usually from three different stores). Laundry has to be done (aprons, tea towels, dishcloths, hot pads). Ingredients have to be prepared ahead of time—measuring into containers, chopping, slicing, and so on. Starting three hours before class, the room needs to be prepped—ingredient trays finalized; iced tea and coffee made; napkins, plates, and recipes set out; rest rooms checked for cleanliness and supplies; microphone tested; candles lit.

That's all before a class meeting, and the list of details keeps growing when you add after-class and between-class chores. The point is that as hardworking as Judie is, she simply can't do it by herself. Her assistants' help is essential.

I certainly saw this in the restaurant business as well. Customers come in waves every day at the usual times—breakfast, lunch, and dinner—and you'd better be ready. If you're not, it's panic city when the people start arriving; if you are, it's fun to watch as hundreds of folks are served smoothly and efficiently. Your staff lays the foundation in the off-peak times for making those customers happy. That's when they have the opportunity to roll silverware in napkins; prepare the batter for your chicken-fried steak; peel, cut up, and cook potatoes for "real" mashed potatoes; bake the fresh bread; and so on.

As the owner/manager, you could never do all that by yourself. But a hardworking crew that has taken advantage of the slow times can actually make the rush hours fun.

Following are a few tips to help make your leadership endeavors successful by surrounding yourself with good people and appreciating their expertise.

Hire People Who Produce Results, Not Excuses

Since no leader is an island, to paraphrase the poem, it's vital that you hire good people: hard workers, people of strong character, people who share the firm's sense of mission, skilled workers, people to whom you can delegate tasks with a high level of confidence that they will get the job done.

How do you find such people? First, look for people who are willing to accept responsibility not just for themselves, but also for the welfare of the business. These people understand that the buck stops with them, that if anything needs to be fixed in their department, it's up to them to see that it happens. They produce results, not excuses.

Second, look for people who are excited about the work, who are motivated primarily by the desire to help provide your organization's products and services. People whose primary motivation is money will be dedicated more to their pocketbooks than to your cause.

Third, offer good salaries so that good and talented workers will be drawn to your firm. If possible, pay more than your competition, and offer better incentives and working conditions. The best thing you can do for yourself is to hire top-notch people to labor with you.

Finally, make prayer a part of your hiring process. This seems so obvious, as it applies to every aspect of life, but as Scripture points out, "Man looks at the outward appearance, but the LORD looks at the heart" (1 Sam. 16:7). Praying and entrusting your personnel decisions to him can also promote a mind and heart at rest.

Expect the Best, but Plan for the Worst

The world's wisest man wrote that "there is a time for everything . . . a time to weep and a time to laugh, a time to mourn and a time to dance" (Eccles. 3:1, 4). That's true on a personal level—trials and tragedies (as well as joys) come into every life—and it's also true on the corporate level. Every enterprise will have times of struggle, periods when things go wrong and its very survival may be on the line.

The same wise man said that "plans fail for lack of counsel, but with many advisers they succeed" (Prov. 15:22). That's true as well, and by following this counsel from God's Book, a leader can cooperate with his Spirit in creating considerable serenity. Let me explain what I mean.

Knowing that tough times are inevitable, a leader can enlist "many advisers"—his or her senior staff—in developing a crisis management plan. Such a plan, if built properly, can make maneuvering through challenging situations, rather than defaulting to panic mode, possible.

In our chocolate company, we pulled together the senior people from all departments: purchasing, manufacturing, accounting, sales, shipping, and so forth. We asked, "From the perspective of your responsibility, what are the different things that could go wrong?" Then we asked, for each of those things, "If that were to happen, what would be the impact on your area?" Next we asked, "What can we do now to cushion those impacts or avoid them altogether if the bad events occur?"

In the accounting area, for instance, one of the worst-case scenarios was that in economically tough times, our customers could start taking longer to pay their bills—maybe a lot longer. And if our customers didn't pay us, how would we pay *our* bills?

What could we do to prepare for that situation? One answer was that in good times, we could channel part of our profits into a reserve fund. We would leave that account alone until we needed it to help carry us through periods of slow cash flow. Another answer was—again in the good times, before we needed them—to establish lines of credit with our bankers so that we could quickly borrow funds to meet short-term demand.

In the purchasing and manufacturing areas, the leaders said that while they could buy sugar from many different sources, meaning we should be okay if one supplier cut us off for some reason, chocolate was another story. Different suppliers sold different blends with differing tastes, and the number of suppliers for our particular blend was limited. What if our main source couldn't get the product or went bankrupt?

How could we plan to maintain an uninterrupted supply of the right chocolate? As the team explored and discussed possibilities, one answer was to find at least three suppliers of our blend and start spreading our business between them. That way, if a problem arose with one source, we would still have two or more others to rely upon.

Any of those vendors would have loved to have all our business. Buying from just one, we also could have secured better prices. But the security and peace of mind that came with having multiple vendors, our team agreed, was worth the extra cost.

In this same way, we worked through all the scenarios, drawing on the experience and expertise of our senior staff. The result was a plan that gave us a little more confidence: We could weather most economic storms that might arise.

Control Debt; Sleep Well

A friend told me years ago, "Only borrow as much as will allow you to sleep peacefully." Experience has shown me that that's some of the best advice I've ever received.

The dangers of getting deep in debt when your firm is struggling are obvious. The dangers are more subtle, and thus even more of a threat to your tranquility (not to mention your solvency), when the organization is doing well.

Sales are going well, and new opportunities are on the horizon, so you need more supplies now, even though all the money isn't in the bank at the moment. You could sell even more if you expanded capacity, but that means more equipment, more staff, and maybe also a bigger plant and a bigger warehouse. You could open up more sales territories, but you'd need more marketing and sales people and an expanded support crew, not to mention a larger advertising budget.

Rapid growth, overoptimism, ego, greed—any one of these can fuel a decision to borrow. Then, if a major account drops you, if the economy turns sour and your product or service is seen as more luxury than necessity, if someone chips a tooth on a pecan shell in one of your candies or if any of a thousand other things goes wrong, suddenly your projections are doubtful and you might have a debt you can't repay.

Scripture says, "The borrower is servant to the lender" (Prov. 22:7). Miss a payment or two on your corporate debt and you'll quickly discover just how true that is.

Here again, others can be a big help. Your bankers will counsel caution; listen to them. Your own accounting people will make conservative estimates of sales and cash flow; you might be frustrated at times, but going with their numbers could save you later. And for sure, listen to that little voice in the back of your head, the one that determines how well you sleep.

Let Other Experts Lead You

Only a fool would think that only he or she has good ideas about how to run an organization. Real wisdom lies in identifying firms that do certain things well, learning all you can about how they do it, and comparing their methods to your own. This is called benchmarking.

Does one of your competitors, for instance, do an outstanding job of inventory control? Discover all you can about his or her keys to success, and talk with your team about how to adapt them to your operation.

My wife, Judie, and I once went on a culinary tour, searching for ideas on how to give a fresh look to her cooking school. Her sole approach at the time was to have students come in for a single two-and-a-half- to three-hour seminar. As we talked with a woman who had a cooking school in France, we learned that her business model was to have students come for an entire week.

This more-extended period allowed for visits to various restaurant kitchens, even to local farms. It made bringing in adjunct instructors to teach their specialties more practical. Though this plan accommodated fewer students, each of them paid considerably more for the experience than Judie was getting for her one-shot seminars.

The bottom line: This French school owner could generate in eight weeks the same revenue that it would take Judie twenty weeks to earn. By benchmarking her operation against this very different but highly successful model, Judie obtained all kinds of fresh and tested ideas for her school.

Though the temptation to try to go it alone can be strong, there's great wisdom in learning from others' success. Getting good people on your team and letting them help to carry the load means much more work will get done, everyone will be happier, and your sleep will be far more restful.

Can You Taste Success?

1. What are some details of your job that you could delegate to others?
2. In light of what you've read in this chapter, what changes might you want to make in how you evaluate potential employees?
3. What are your current plans for dealing with possible crises in your business? What changes or additions might you need to make?
4. Does your firm's debt level allow you to sleep well at night? Why or why not? If not, what steps could you take to reduce debt?
5. Name three other organizations you could use to benchmark various parts of your operation. If you can't name three, do some research to find three over the next thirty days.

NEVER REST ON YOUR LAURELS

You can't take a break when cooking caramels for chocolate centers. You have to keep the caramel at an exact temperature every minute so it doesn't stiffen, stay too sticky, or become grainy.

In the same way, the winning leader stays attentive and gently stirs an organization's smooth progress.

Our chocolate company found itself working with a major department store chain whose business was going exceedingly well. Sales were so good, in fact, that the top management decided to expand greatly over the next five years, adding a number of new stores.

To make this happen, they believed that they needed to focus almost all the corporate attention on the growth plans for that period. The buyer we worked with, who bought for all their stores, went so far as to tell me that because he would be concentrating on stocking all those new stores, he would depend on our company and his other suppliers to keep stock up to par in the existing stores.

It amazed me to think that they would give so much control over their inventory to suppliers. That was my first thought. My second was that this was probably not a good sign in the long run—that this successful organization seemed prepared to rest on its laurels in its existing stores, subjecting them to a sort of benign neglect.

Well, the good news is that in the short term, with us vendors keeping a close eye on their supplies of our products, those existing stores soon came to be better stocked than they had been in the recent past.

The bad news, though, is that the employees in those stores quickly picked up on the corporate attitude of complacency. And when that happened, they reflected that neglect in the way they worked.

Staff members no longer kept product on the shelves neat and in order.

Floors and fixtures didn't get dusted and shined as frequently.

The sales staff no longer emphasized complete, courteous attention to customers.

As you walked through one of these stores, you noticed that things just weren't as sharp, as pristine, as "cut above the rest" as before.

Not surprisingly, this corporate laziness gradually began to make an impact on their sales. We watched with concern as our business with them first plateaued and then actually started to fall. They noticed, too. One year into the plan, one of their buyers told me, "You know, we were making more profit with fewer stores than we are now with all these new stores."

Fortunately, the chain was big enough and had sufficient reserves to survive the downturn. After about two years, its leaders realized they could not keep presuming upon the goodwill of their customers. They hired some additional help to focus on getting their existing stores back in shape, doing those little things that had built their business in the first place. And with time, effort, and diligent oversight, they managed to turn things around.

Success can obviously be a great blessing. But it also brings with it some serious dangers. One of the worst is the tendency to rest on your laurels—to get lazy. To think that now you've got it made, you've reached the top, so you can relax. This tendency is like a virus that can infect individual leaders, management teams and boards of directors, even whole organizations.

Succumb to this toxin and—if you don't recognize the danger and get help in time—your enterprise will get sicker and sicker until it surely dies.

As the opening story shows, a little success brings with it the potential for danger, and great success can foster catastrophic harm to an organization.

Part of the danger is that any enterprise with a bit of success can slide into complacency so easily. What's the harm in letting up just a bit? You've earned that privilege, right? So what if the merchandise isn't quite as neat and carefully arranged on the shelves as in the past? It's no big deal to the customers, is it? So what if the sales clerks aren't quite as friendly and attentive as in days gone by? The customers know us and love us! So what if a little trash gathers on the carpet and dust accumulates on the fixtures? Nobody will notice, right?

And so, little by little, the standards of quality and service slip. But people *do* notice and *do* care, the company's reputation is tarnished, and competitors start to look more appealing to the paying customers.

The truly successful leader remains constantly aware of this danger, however, and guards himself and his team against it. He never lapses into laziness but disciplines himself to do the daily work necessary to maintain the highest standards. And he makes sure that others in the firm don't get sloppy either.

Manage Yourself First

What I'm talking about here is simple self-control. That is, the *concept* is simple. Actually exercising self-control—disciplining ourselves to do the things needed to stay on top of our jobs, and to fulfill our responsibilities as leaders every day—is extremely challenging and sometimes impossible on our own.

That's why the Scriptures say, "He who rules his spirit [is better] than he who takes [i.e., conquers militarily] a city" (Prov. 16:32 ESV). And that's because keeping yourself under control at all times is even harder than conquering a fortified city!

Looking at the matter from the negative point of view, the Scriptures say, "A man without self-control is like a city broken into and left without walls" (Prov. 25:28 ESV). In other words, that person is defenseless, vulnerable to any and all sorts of danger.

Once again, as with the other concepts in this book, the key to being able to demonstrate self-control consistently is to live in harmony with, and in reliance upon, God's Spirit. When, for instance, my inclination is to act rashly out of fear or some other emotion, or to be lazy and sloppy in my work, he motivates and empowers me to do the right thing.

Just what sorts of things does a leader need to attend to day in and day out to keep complacency from creeping in? Here are a few tips.

Keep a Steady Eye on Key Numbers

In any organization, a few key budget figures reveal the essence of how you're doing financially. When sales are good and profits are rolling in, it's easy to take your eye off these details and just figure that, as Shakespeare put it, "All's well that ends well." It's a little laziness that can turn into a big mistake over time.

In the restaurant business, the three key numbers are revenue, food costs, and labor costs. For our chicken-fried steak house, we budgeted food to take about 30 percent of income.

At every weekly management meeting, we checked all three numbers. Even when sales were strong and the bottom line looked healthy, we wanted to make sure our costs stayed in line.

Well, one week we noticed that food costs were up to 35 percent. The manager had some reasonable explanation for the variance, so we let it go. The next week food was above normal again, but the manager again had a reason: heavy buying for a big catering job or some such. "Okay," we said, "but keep an eye on those costs."

The week following that, though the bottom line was still okay, food costs had climbed to 37 percent. Then we had a pattern that we couldn't overlook, and if this kept up, we'd soon be losing money regardless of how strong sales were. We told the manager he'd better investigate.

He took the warning seriously and made the time to look into the problem. At our next meeting, he reported that he'd had to let one of the cooks go, because the man had been taking home meat out of the freezer. The week after that, our food costs were back in line.

Resist the Temptation to Let Quality Slide

Besides watching the numbers, a diligent leader also has to make sure that the company's products and services remain at the highest level of quality.

In our restaurant, we constantly monitored the ingredients for our signature chicken-fried steak to make sure we had the freshest meat (except for the one week, mentioned elsewhere, when we tried frozen and pre-breaded meat), in extra large portions, along with fresh spices for our batter and gravy. We carefully trained all new kitchen staff in how to prepare the food and display it on the plate. We thoroughly trained all wait staff in how to greet and treat customers.

I'm convinced that if we hadn't stayed on top of these details and kept our quality from slipping even a little, our competition could have eaten us alive (no pun intended).

Find New Ways to Win Customers

Of course, while maintaining standards with core goods and services, a successful leader also has to anticipate changes in the marketplace. He has to lead the team in planning for and developing new products to keep customers coming back.

Prior to the 1990s, our chocolate company had sold exclusively to high-end department stores, a few midlevel department stores, and better gift shops. In all three places, we sold only a premium quality candy line. But our marketing and sales staffs saw that more and more people were shopping in discount stores. Could top-level store accounts alone keep our company growing? And if we continued to ignore the discounters, wouldn't we be missing out on millions of potential consumers?

So, starting in 1991, we began to develop what we called a Middle American line with a lower price point. (Although you'll see in other chapters that there were problems with the way we went about it, the basic idea was good.) We also entered the discount store market with some discontinued product lines. In both cases, we got excellent results.

My guiding philosophy in thinking about what we need to be doing next is this: Always solve a problem before it becomes a problem.

In 1991, our sales of top-drawer chocolates to top-level stores were still strong. We didn't *have* to make changes at that point. But the market trend was clearly moving in favor of the midlevel and discount stores, and it looked as if it might be a permanent shift. If we began to adjust then, we stood a good chance of being able to supply all the markets, as opposed to waiting and watching while our one existing market started to dwindle. (I'll say more about the need to pursue new ideas in chapter 10.)

Avoid the Quick Fix

Speaking of solving problems before they become bigger problems, another time when leaders are prone to laziness, at least mentally, is when their enterprise is struggling financially. They can't buy the materials they need, or they may not make payroll at the end of the week. In such situations, the easy, knee-jerk response is to go to the bank and try to get a loan.

That approach leaves you deeper in debt and still saddled with whatever troubles that turned your organization into a money loser.

The tough but better response is to roll up your sleeves, dig into the situation, find the core problems, and take whatever actions you need to reduce expenses, generate more revenue, and turn things around.

Choose Consistency over Flash

The business world, and especially the investment world, focuses—obsesses, really—on how a company did in the latest quarter and where the stock price is today. It lionizes the leader who can make a powerful presentation and preside smoothly over a press conference.

In my view, however, the truly successful leader is the consistent performer who never takes a day off in terms of effort, never grows complacent, maybe doesn't even say much in meetings, but just gets the job done at the highest level year after year.

We had a woman on our senior staff who ran the manufacturing operation. A person of few words, Betsy nonetheless kept things moving more smoothly than in any other plant I've ever seen. Even when she did speak up in a staff meeting, she spoke quietly and sparingly—but other employees rarely challenged her ideas. Simply put, with Betsy in charge, I didn't worry about whether the factory was getting its work done.

I asked her one time, "Betsy, which would you say is more important: your preparation work for the day ahead or the out-front supervision you do once the line is running?"

Without hesitation she replied, "Preparation is far more important. If I've done that right—we've set the priorities, we've got raw materials on hand, the equipment is ready to go, and the line people and forepeople have been given clear instructions—the supervisory stuff is easy."

"How many hours do you spend on each part of the job in a typical day?" I asked.

"I put in three hours of prep time for every hour I spend on the floor," she said.

Now, if some business news film crew had come to our plant to do a story on what made it so well run, its members would have wanted to capture Betsy walking the floor—*not* calling inventory early that morning to make sure her people had the ingredients they needed for the day.

They would've wanted her pondering with furrowed brow how to get the line going again after a key piece of equipment broke down—*not* working with a maintenance guy before the line workers ever showed up to make sure the machine *wouldn't* break down.

They would have liked to catch her changing plans on the fly midday when a big new order came in—*not* checking with the sales manager late the previous night so she'd know the demands she'd be facing the next morning.

No, Betsy's way of working wasn't exciting and wouldn't make great television. She just kept our factory running at the peak of efficiency day after day, month after month, and year after year. She led by example and with compassion, and her team responded with loyalty and hard work.

119

Don't Cram; Diligently Prepare

A leader who's not resting on his laurels also does his homework before making a presentation in a meeting. A lazy or complacent leader thinks he can just breeze through and still carry the day.

I'll never forget the first time I applied for a business loan. Our company was doing pretty well, but we needed some extra cash to fuel our growth while waiting for accounts receivable to come in. (That's the right time to borrow.) Of course, going into the meeting with the commercial banker, I knew he'd want to see a business plan. So I drew one up.

Since our balance sheet looked good, I figured getting the loan was a foregone conclusion, a no-brainer for the bank. So, frankly, I didn't put much time or effort into writing the business plan. I hastily pulled some numbers out of my head, for things like future sales, that I thought would give the bank a good impression of our thriving business—almost pie in the sky.

Well, to my surprise, as the banker read through my plan that afternoon, he was *not* impressed. And he asked such bothersome questions as, "If your sales fall 15 percent below these very optimistic projections, how would you repay our loan?"

Of course, I had no solid explanations for those optimistic numbers in my plan. Of course, I had no good answers for his annoying, though perfectly reasonable (in retrospect), questions.

And, of course, I walked out of the bank with no loan.

Also, of course, I have never walked into another banker's office without having first done my homework, nailed my numbers, and prepared myself to answer well any question he or she might possibly ask.

Read to Lead

Finally, he who reads, leads. A leader simply can't ever afford to think he or she knows it all and can, therefore, stop making the time and effort to learn.

The world is constantly changing. New research is being done. New ways of doing business—whole new industries—are invented regularly. A leader who wants to stay on top of his or her field, who wants to help shape a positive future for his or her enterprise rather than always being pressed to react to forces that seem out of control, must read.

None of these steps is optional, "Maybe I'll get to it after I've done everything else on my list" activity. They are all vital parts of the work of a leader who is never content to rest on his or her past accomplishments—a truly successful leader.

Can You Taste Success?

1. How good are you at disciplining yourself? Be as candid as you can. How can you grow in this vital area?
2. What are the key numbers in your area of responsibility? How carefully do you watch them?

3. In your work, would you describe yourself more as consistent or as flashy? Why? What changes might you want to make in this regard?
4. On a grading scale from A to F, how well do you do the homework necessary to your position? What steps can you take to earn an A?
5. In your work, would you call yourself a reader? Why or why not?

EARN CREDIBILITY EVERY DAY

Making first-rate cherry cordials requires faithfulness to the process. A cherry center is encased in a solid coating called sucrovert that takes two weeks to break down and liquefy after being covered in chocolate. No matter how strong the demand or short the supply, maintaining a reputation for quality cherry cordials means waiting for this seasoning process to occur.

So it is that the winning leader sees and values how the process of good decision making, investments, and interactions every day adds up to desired results.

Tim was part of our senior staff, and through him I learned a vital lesson in leadership. As operations vice president, Tim was incredibly diligent and reliable. With him in charge, you knew projects would get completed and the plant would be put to bed properly at the end of the day. There wasn't a person on earth I would have had more confidence in—even though his methods and mine were totally opposite.

Most people fall into one of two categories: They're either "big picture" or "detail oriented." The first group—to which I belong—are your optimists, your dreamers, your "Sure, we can do that!" cheerleaders. The second—to which Tim belonged—are your self-labeled "realists," your "We need to find the pitfalls in this scheme" skeptics.

You can imagine how a "dreamer's" cavalier attitude about the daily grind might drive a "detailer" crazy, and vice versa. My type can easily come across as shallow, inexact, and too pie-in-the-sky. Tim's type can come across as negative—a real no-no—to someone like me.

Tim and I butted heads many times over our differences in mind-set and approach, creating great irritation on both sides.

Then one night as I lay awake thinking of Tim and our conflicts, a thought hit me like a Mack truck: Here it was midnight, and I could say without doubt that I knew the factory doors were securely locked and the operations safely put to bed. If there had been anything wrong at the end of the day, Tim would have seen it and taken care of it.

The sense of security that gave me was priceless.

After this midnight epiphany, I realized that I needed to better understand and respect Tim's modus operandi. Furthermore, I needed to earn credibility with him by letting go and allowing him to do things his way. If I could learn to appreciate his personality and ways, even though they were so different from mine, our working relationship could grow by leaps and bounds.

In the months that followed, I learned that the dreamer needs the realist to balance him out. I tend to always see the glass as half full. And that's fine; it creates energy and excitement in the organization. But by itself it can lead to poor decisions and methods. On the other hand, with someone like Tim providing the balance, that energy can be channeled for consistent growth.

Because we were opposites, we forced each other to constantly double-check our attitudes and methods. Was I moving too quickly? Was he moving fast enough? We still sometimes "duked it out" over details, but I had come to realize that this was a good thing, not a bad thing.

If you allow your differences to be positives instead of negatives, and you learn to work with that person who's so different from you, you can earn enormous credibility as a leader who deserves to be followed.

When you make a point of earning credibility with your staff every day, you build trust. When you don't, eventually everything will fall apart around you. That's where my company would have headed if I had clung to the idea that the plant manager needed to be just like me.

Working to merit credibility day after day, realizing that you can never take a day off, calls for *faithfulness*—to your team and to your role as a leader.

Whenever you wonder whether you've got credibility as a leader, ask yourself two questions: First, when you're not around, do your staffers work as hard as they would if you were there, or do they start to slack off? If they respect you as a person and a boss, they won't want you to be disappointed when you return. Second, when you look back over your shoulder, how many people do you see following you? That is, how many share your vision and goals and are giving their best effort consistently in the hope of helping you reach those objectives?

If you can honestly and realistically give positive answers to both of those questions, you've earned a lot of credibility with your crew. They *believe* in you. God's Spirit is helping you to be faithful to your calling, even when you don't feel like doing it. But if your objective answers are less than reassuring, your credibility needs serious shoring up.

Earn Credibility by Making People Your Priority

How does a leader earn credibility with those who are supposed to be following? Over the years, I've learned that the answer has several parts, but they're all summarized in this one key thought: *Put people first, then product.*

If you do that every day, you'll have credibility *and* success. If you don't, you'll have neither.

If that looks like something you've read before in this book, you're right. It's a recurring theme because it's so important.

But what does it mean to put people first, in the context of earning credibility? It sounds simple, perhaps even simplistic. I can assure you, however, that it's not simple—and even more, it's not easy. Let me explain just what it involves.

Specifically, earning credibility by putting people first calls for the following steps:

1. **Appreciate and respect all kinds of people**, not just people who are like you. Don't show favoritism toward like-minded folks, either.
2. **Lead more than you manage** (the topic of chapter 2). Pursue effectiveness more than efficiency. An effective leader concentrates on doing the right things; an efficient, managerial mind-set person concentrates on doing things right—a vital distinction.
3. **Refuse to give in to, and to act upon, damaging emotions** such as greed, envy, and pride.
4. **Honor the values your people bring to the workplace.** They want to be recognized, respected, and rewarded. They want to be able to take pride in what they do. And they want the freedom to make choices (within reason).
5. **Make your plans carefully before announcing them.** Your staff will recognize half-baked ideas when they hear them, and you never get a second chance to make a first impression.

Those are the components. Now let me unpack what each of them means.

1. Appreciate and Respect All Kinds of People

As my experience with Tim, the operations v.p., and his successor shows, it takes all kinds of people to make a successful organization. I could tell numerous similar stories, because the lesson didn't sink in right away.

There was, for example, the time I started the home-style restaurant I mentioned in earlier chapters and hired a glass-half-full manager like myself. Ron was great at such big-picture tasks as developing our theme and coming up with new ideas for decorating and for the menu. When it came to the daily details of running the business, though—that was another story.

I remember especially how we brainstormed plans for a catering side of the restaurant and then put a lot of money and effort into promoting it. We got a good response, too, from people who had tried our food and liked what we had to offer. But when it came to implementation, Ron was soon letting details slip and costing us a lot of business.

The bottom line for catering customers is that they want you to show up early, with everything you need in hand. Otherwise, they quickly start to panic, afraid you're going to ruin their event. Ron, however, could never seem to get his team and the food together quite on time, let alone early. And once he got to the location, he was often missing something important, forcing a staff person to race back to the restaurant. Meanwhile, the customer was breaking out in a cold sweat.

Eventually, in an effort to salvage the catering business, I had to replace Ron with a glass-half-empty, take-care-of-the-details kind of manager. This guy had a checklist for everything, and he was soon earning kudos from satisfied customers.

Those who are critical and who obsess over details make good accountants, inventory managers, quality control people, contract managers, and customer service representatives, to name just a few positions where they excel. Those who dream big and have never met an insurmountable obstacle make good planners, salespeople, and public relations representatives, to name some of the things they do well.

Another broad way to look at people is that some are givers and some are takers. We might tend to think that a staff made up of nothing but givers would be a good thing. But takers, who tend to refuse to accept no as a final answer, fill a needed role and deserve respect, too—sometimes it takes such a person to kick open a door of opportunity or to deal with unreasonable parties (always with respect, of course).

Your job and mine as leaders is to recognize our team members' skills and basic outlooks on life, then put them into positions where they can contribute the most and achieve the greatest success, both personally and for the organization. That's being faithful to the way God made them as individuals. And the time and effort we put into finding a good fit for each staffer will be repaid many times over.

2. Lead More Than You Manage

Leaders tend to ask, "Are we focusing our time and effort on the things that are most important to achieving our objectives?" Those with a managerial mind-set—

whether they're CEOs or midlevel executives—tend to ask, "Are we doing things the way we're supposed to, 'by the book'?" In other words, leaders pursue effectiveness—doing the right things that lead to success—while the managerial mind-setters pursue efficiency—doing things well, whether or not they're the best things to be doing.

That's a vital distinction, and workers recognize the difference. They will follow a leader, trusting that he or she is in tune with what's best for the team. When a leader says, "We need to do A," the staff will believe it and work hard at A. That's credibility.

One way to lead in this regard is with a mission statement that paints a clear picture in everyone's mind of what the team is trying to accomplish. It should also, if possible, stir the emotions and inspire hope and a sense of purpose. And once you have written it, you should hold it up before the staff continually, reminding them that they're all part of an exciting, worthwhile enterprise.

A good example of this is Dr. James Dobson's Focus on the Family ministry, which puts new employees through a full-day orientation their first day on the job. In the morning, they take care of such basic necessities as explaining benefits and filling out insurance forms. But in the afternoon, the human resources people review the organization's many activities and how they help people, giving the new staff a sense of being part of a grand and noble cause. They challenge the new crew members to dedicate themselves to excellence and teamwork in service to that cause. By the end of the day, even such behind-the-scenes staff as accountants and custodians leave with the feeling that they play a vital part in the success of this important endeavor.

Then, every few years after employees join the team, they undergo a day's worth of philosophy training. In that program, they hear again why the organization exists, what values underlie its mission, and what enduring objectives will ultimately define true success. Through the course of the day, they hear many true stories of people whom different parts of the ministry have aided.

The result is that everyone understands the "big picture" and his or her part in it, and has confidence that the leaders—whatever their faults—are nonetheless steering the organization in a good direction. They see that the whole team is being faithful to its stated mission, and they go back to work with a renewed spirit of commitment.

3. Refuse to Give In to, and Act upon, Damaging Emotions

All of us have emotions, including some that come from our darker side, such as greed, envy, and pride. We can't help what we feel, but we can decide how we're going to act. We can choose, with God's help, whether or not to give in to those damaging emotions. A leader who wants to put people first and earn credibility with them will choose not to give in.

I remember one sales manager, Larry, who got so psyched up before customer meetings that he was almost falling off his chair with excitement. Then, when he made his presentations, he was so caught up in pride, greed, and the desire to "win" that he gave the buyer almost anything to make the sale.

I especially recall the time when Larry made a large sale to a major chain of stores by giving the buyer a 20 percent discount—much higher than our norm—"just to get our foot in the door," as he put it. At the time he felt great because he had "won." But by discounting our product so much, we broke even at best on the deal. Big sale; no profit.

When Larry's crew heard what he had done, they shook their heads and groaned. Because he had let his emotions carry him away, they would find it difficult to ever make a profit from this new customer. And when other customers heard about the deal (that kind of news always gets around somehow), they would start asking why they couldn't have the same terms.

In other words, Larry's lack of emotional control meant nothing but headaches for the rest of his team. He had won in the short term, but in the long term his crew paid for it.

His credibility with them, like the company's profit, was about zero.

If you want to be a winning leader, commit instead to being the hardest worker and most dedicated team player in the place. Even when you feel tired, stressed out, unappreciated, frustrated, or deserving of special treatment, don't ask anyone to do something that you're not willing to do yourself. And never let greed drive you to do something that will make you look good for a while but will hurt those looking to you for leadership.

In short, no matter what you're feeling, let the Spirit guide and strengthen you to be faithful in your role—to do what's best for those under and around you. Discipline your desires. Remember that leadership is much more a responsibility than a privilege. You're there to serve, not to be served.

4. *Honor the Values Your People Bring to the Workplace*

Honoring people more than money also means respecting the values that your staffers bring to the workplace. Jesus captured this idea in words when he told us, "So in everything, do to others what you would have them do to you" (Matt. 7:12). That's the Golden Rule again, which I referred to earlier.

What values do I mean? People want to be treated with respect and dignity, including getting fair pay and having working conditions that are as pleasant as the nature of the work allows.

As much as the job permits—and that's usually much more than most leaders think it is—they want personal choice and freedom to do the work their way.

They want to have the time and resources to do the best job of which they're capable, so they can take pride in their work.

When they do good work and accomplish or exceed their goals, they want to be recognized for it.

If a leader honors these values faithfully—day in and day out—so that the staff members feel respected, free, appreciated, and proud of their accomplishments, they will respect him, trust him, and bend over backward to help the team succeed.

In our chocolate factory, 85 percent of the employees were women. Most were mothers with children still living at home. As I talked with these women, I picked up on the fact that some were coming to work with family concerns on their minds.

The root cause was that the standard 8:00 to 5:00 workday interfered with their ability to meet their kids' needs. Some had children who needed to be at soccer practice at 4:30. Others had children whose school day started at 8:30, and those moms wanted to be able to spend an organized morning with their kids and then drive them to school.

As I listened, it dawned on me that if these women could feel better about meeting their children's needs, not only would their families benefit, but they would also be more productive at work.

So I met with my human resources people, and we devised a plan for flexible working schedules that allowed people to do a good job for us *and* better meet their other obligations. We also instituted job sharing for those who could work only part-time. Now their minds could be on the job at hand and not on worry over whether their kids would get to soccer practice.

Bottom line: The work still got done, better than ever. The people were happy and productive. I gained credibility by having shown greater sensitivity to their values—by treating them as I would want to be treated in their position. And the company prospered.

5. Make Your Plans Carefully before Announcing Them

Jesus also said, "Suppose one of you wants to build a tower. Will he not first sit down and estimate the cost to see if he has enough money to complete it? For if he lays the foundation and is not able to finish it, everyone who sees it will ridicule him, saying, 'This fellow began to build and was not able to finish'" (Luke 14:28–30).

In leadership terms, the lesson is that if you gain a reputation with your staff members for announcing ill-advised plans, which they then have to overhaul at great cost in time, effort, and money halfway into the campaign or project—if you're not faithful to your responsibility to do your homework and make good plans before launching out in a new direction—your crew will soon learn to greet your next big idea, not with enthusiasm and confidence, but with a roll of the eyes and a shake of the head. Their commitment to the plan will be lukewarm at best, and it will show in the work they do.

This is another lesson I learned the hard way.

From boyhood, I had loved the outdoors, farms—the whole America-the-beautiful and apple pie scene. I had never lived on a farm, but I had surely idealized and fantasized about what it would be like to own and operate one.

Well, after I had bought my own chocolate factory, I figured I then had my opportunity to buy a dairy. My rationalization was that it would be great to have a direct source of cream—straight from the cow, as it were—pasteurized for safety but otherwise not processed. The result would be a unique and better-tasting chocolate.

At root, though, this was an emotional decision, not a well-thought-out plan. I couldn't see that, but my staff could. When I announced my brilliant idea, they let out a collective groan.

If I had been in a frame of mind to listen and accept advice, they would have said, "What do you or we know about running a dairy?" and "Isn't it a lot cheaper and

easier to get our milk and cream from existing farms?"
But I wasn't in that frame of mind, and besides, I was
confident my plan would work. So I pushed the idea
through.

Soon I was playing the part of Farmer Bill, and almost
as soon I was discovering that there's nothing romantic
about running a dairy farm.

You have to get up mighty early to see that your cows
are milked. And you have to do it *every* day: no weekends off, no holidays, no vacations. I tried to teach my
cows that Sunday, at least, was a day of rest, but they
didn't go for it.

I didn't fare any better with running the business side
of the dairy. I really didn't know what I was doing. And
because I had rushed into the deal on an emotional
basis, I also had failed to get it financed on favorable
terms. Bottom line: We never did make any money, and
it eventually began bleeding red ink.

By the time our losses had hit five digits, and I had
worn myself to a frazzle trying to run the dairy on top
of my other responsibilities, I had to admit defeat and
pull the plug. I could no longer avoid the reality that my
team had seen as inevitable from the start.

When I announced the decision, they were generally
gracious about it, though a few couldn't resist poking a
little good-natured fun at my rashness. And from all the
comments I heard, I knew that they had placed me on
a sort of probation in their minds. They were thinking,
*Has he learned his lesson, or will his next big idea be just
as harebrained as this one?*

I resolved then and there not to repeat the mistakes
that had led to my farming folly; I would ram no more

half-baked plans down the throats of people I paid to give me good counsel.

I'm glad to say that for the most part I've kept that resolve. But do you know what? *I've never been able to completely live down my dairy disaster.*

Take it from me, then: Before you finalize and announce plans, make sure that you're doing the right things, in the right way, for the right reasons. Seek and listen to wise and godly counsel, for "plans fail for lack of counsel, but with many advisers they succeed" (Prov. 15:22).

In other words, be faithful to your planning responsibilities as a leader. Your people want to know that you've done *your* job before you ask them to do theirs.

They want you to show that you respect their time and talent by making sure you won't be wasting either before you give them their marching orders.

They want to know that you won't require them to go above and beyond the call of duty just to cover your backside and the fact that you weren't diligent in your work as a leader.

Earning credibility with your staff is a daily requirement. A leader's every word, decision, and action either increases or diminishes it. When he or she has earned and is earning credibility, people are willing to work incredibly hard and well to help the organization fulfill its mission.

On the other hand, when a leader fails to earn credibility, that lack of trust and confidence will eat away at morale and at the team's spirit. It will erode respect for the leader and the willingness to follow. Unchecked over time, it will render the leader a boss in name only.

That's why leaders need to be in step with the Spirit, allowing him to produce faithfulness in their lives. The result is a consistency and a dependability in putting your people first and watching your credibility and success soar.

Can You Taste Success?

1. Are you a glass-half-full or a glass-half-empty type of person? How well do you appreciate and respect people of the other type?
2. What do you and your organization do to remind your staff of the corporate mission? What more might you do to help them keep it in mind?
3. How much of a role do your emotions play in the decisions you make? Is that a good thing or a bad thing? Why?
4. Based on what you've read in this chapter, how well are you honoring your employees' values? How could you do a better job of that?
5. What plans for a new project, product, or system do you currently have in the works? How carefully have you thought them through?

WELCOME SMALL FAILURES

In days gone by, hand-dippers artfully strung melted chocolate on top of each piece as a clue to what filling lay at the center. For instance, a lightning streak marked a maple-flavored truffle, three dots flagged a caramel center, and a sweeping S meant strawberry crème. As such marking has become a dying art, you may now bite into what you think is a caramel only to discover it's a vanilla nougat. Or your peanut cluster might actually prove to be laced with raisins, not nuts.

Just as some of these surprises can be delicious discoveries, small failures in business can turn you onto something new, more pleasing, and better for all.

L ike most leaders who hire staff for their enterprises, I've always wanted to provide work for handicapped people if we could find good job fits. Over the course of several years in the chocolate factory, we tried out people with different types of limitations. For example, we made the effort to train some folks with mental challenges, some who were wheelchair bound, and so on.

Unfortunately, even though we walked the extra mile to try to help these employees succeed, things just never went well. The combination of physical and mental demands was more than they could handle. As hard as they tried, and as hard as we tried to help them become productive workers, one after another failed to get up to speed, got discouraged, and left.

My employment staff and I grew discouraged as well. Maybe the types of jobs we had to offer were simply not conducive to our using handicapped people. As much as we wanted to help and be helped by that segment of the community, we almost reached the point of giving up on the idea.

Then one day a young woman named Brenda showed up at our employment office. She seemed bright and eager to work. We had one concern, though, and it was a biggie in light of our experience: Brenda was deaf.

Did we really want to go to the extra effort again to train a handicapped person, only to get frustrated ourselves and probably break her heart when it didn't work out? Most of the staff involved in the decision said no, let's not put ourselves and her through that.

Still, Brenda had some quality, a spark, that we found appealing. Coupled with our desire still to find a way to succeed with handicapped workers if we possibly could, we decided to bring her on board.

We started Brenda in the room where staff put finished chocolates into their custom-sized slots in the retail boxes. Not long after, having observed her work for several days, her supervisor noticed that Brenda had great dexterity.

Hmmm. How might Brenda do at hand-dipping chocolates? we wondered when we heard about that. It's one of the most important and most challenging jobs in a factory that makes fine chocolates. The dipping has to be done right so you get consistency in look and in quality, yet it has to be done fairly quickly if the company is going to make a profit.

Well, Brenda took to the job like a bee to a flower. She picked up the techniques almost immediately. She had phenomenal feel. And she wasn't distracted by all the talk and other noises in the room, as other workers were. In just a few weeks, she was turning out almost as many pieces per day as dippers with far more experience.

In short, Brenda became a huge success in one of our key positions!

When we discussed all this with her caseworker from the state, she explained, "Sometimes when a person has lost one of her senses, one or more of the other senses improves dramatically, as if to compensate."

That thought gave us hope that other deaf people might work out as well, and with the caseworker's help, we hired more. I'm pleased to report that they, too, soon developed into highly productive employees. In fact, several were so good that they excelled at whatever we asked of them and still wanted more work.

This story has a happy ending. Our company as a whole, and our other employees individually, benefited from working side by side with these folks who were deaf. But we reached that point only after learning from a series of frustrating failures, and only because some people in our employment office had the patience and wisdom to keep trying.

Most people, unless they're in a truly miserable situation, dislike change. They've found a comfortable level of familiarity, stability, and success in the status quo. They're not too interested in trying new things or new ways of doing the old, because that involves the risk of failure. And failure is bad, right?

Failure is bad for your organization.

Failure is bad for you personally, for your "record," and for your career.

Failure on your part will also make your boss look bad.

The simple and unavoidable facts, however, are that as leaders and as organizations, *we have to try new things, those new efforts will sometimes fail, and in general that's a* good *thing*. Thus, the successful leader learns to accept and even welcome small failures.

We have to try new things because the worlds of business and ministry—customer tastes, competition, the economic climate, and so on—are constantly changing. Decades of experience as an entrepreneur have taught me that there's no such thing as treading water. As an enterprise, you're either moving forward or falling behind. If you're not constantly improving products or service, or introducing new products or services, you're growing stale and starting to sink, and your competition will shoot right past you.

Experience has also taught me that when you try new things, no matter how carefully you've strategized and tested, they will sometimes fail. It's inescapable. You will have overlooked some detail. Some action will produce a result you couldn't have foreseen. Or maybe your estimate of customer/client response was just wrong.

But these failures, unless they're big enough to devastate the entire organization (as my dairy farm folly was), are usually good in that they're learning experiences that teach valuable lessons. Even the big failures provide valuable, if painful, instruction. Indeed, we can learn some vital lessons only through enduring a failure or series of failures.

In the story that opened this chapter, for example, we thought we knew what kinds of handicaps people could have and still be productive employees in our chocolate factory. We had consulted the experts, after all! But only after enduring a string of failures, painful as they were for everyone involved, did we discover the type of physical challenge that was not only compatible with the nature of our work but actually seemed to make a person more capable than usual.

A number of years ago, a good friend and fellow businessman named Tom came to me for advice. He had just experienced the collapse of his business and found himself in bad shape. He hoped I could help him recover and get back on the path to success.

I was happy to oblige. I figured I could shower him with pearls of wisdom. After all, at that time my track record as an entrepreneur was unblemished. One way or another, business had always worked out well for me. Obviously, I knew what I was doing. I had all the answers.

Well, I gave Tom my sage counsel and sent him on his way. Though we didn't discuss the details of what he was doing after that, we stayed in touch, and I noted with satisfaction that over the next few years, business went pretty well for him. I privately patted myself on the back and gave myself a large measure of credit for his success.

Then came my first business failure, and it was a whopper. My company suffered a huge downturn. As you might imagine, the experience was painful, humbling—and enlightening. I realized, for one thing, that I wasn't the business genius that I had supposed myself to be.

About that same time, I had occasion to talk with Tom again, and I asked how he had dealt with his failure. Had my advice helped?

"Actually, I didn't take your advice," he replied with a smile.

"You didn't?" I said, taken aback. "Why not?"

"You were too cocky," he said, grinning even wider. "You told me just to do this and do that, and everything would be fine. It was clear you hadn't really thought it through, because you didn't understand how many different ways even the best plans can go wrong. You needed to have your own failure before you could relate to mine."

He was right, of course, and that's when I started to grasp the teaching value of failure.

Ignore Fear; Embrace Failure

Instead of fearing failure and considering it all bad, I've come to see that as a leader, I need to accept and even embrace it. And I need to encourage my staff to try new things as well, not to let the risk of failure keep them from pursuing good ideas. For all of us, this has meant a major attitude adjustment.

Along with that, I've come to redefine failure. Failure is *not* when you try something new or different and it doesn't work as you'd hoped. That's simply a learning experience. Rather, failure is when you don't even try something new and promising because of fear.

Within reasonable bounds, staffers need the freedom to make decisions and implement changes, to seek out and pursue alternatives to the tried and true, to question the corporate orthodoxy, to break the rules of convention if it's for a good reason—and see what happens.

Working with some great salespeople over the years has shown me that their mind-set is a good example of the attitude required of all successful leaders. Here's what I mean: First, great salespeople have to be willing to take risks—it's the essence of their job. Every time they call on a potential customer, there's a very good chance that they'll hear a no. That can be discouraging, not to mention tough on the ego!

Poor salespeople get discouraged, lose hope, and either muddle along in misery or quit. Great salespeople accept the risk, endure the "failures," and keep pushing through to the rewards.

Second, great salespeople don't take the rejections personally. They understand that a customer's no doesn't mean they're dumb, incompetent, or worthless. If they've done their preparation and made a good presentation, a customer's rejection has to do with the product, the state of the economy, or some other factor outside the salesperson's control. So the great seller has the self-confidence to keep going forward—to look even harder for solutions.

Poor salespeople, on the other hand, take every no as a judgment of their worth. After a string of such customer responses, their self-esteem has been shredded and minced like confetti.

Third, great salespeople refuse to accept failure—a customer's initial no—as final. They believe in what they're selling and that it will help the customer, so their job is to answer questions and objections and overcome obstacles until the customer sees things the same way.

I remember a time when I overheard Keith, our sales vice president, on the phone with the key buyer for a large department store chain. Keith's office was next to mine, and at that point I wasn't on the phone myself or in a meeting, so I had a ringside seat. Our chocolates weren't yet in this chain's stores, and Keith was trying to arrange an appointment to make a presentation and get our foot in the door.

I could tell the conversation wasn't going well. When Keith gave a reason for the buyer to see him, a pause followed while the buyer responded, then Keith followed with yet another reason. The call ended with a subdued good-bye.

As was his habit after a negative call, Keith walked from his desk into the hall and began to pace up and down, thinking through what he and the potential client had said, what he could learn from it, and—as always—what his next move should be. I knew the apparent dead end with this particular prospect would be a huge disappointment to him, though, so I went into the hall to join him.

"What happened, Keith?" I asked. "Did they say no?" That's certainly what it had sounded like from where I sat. But I will never forget his answer.

"Oh, no," he shot back without hesitation and in all earnestness. "They just delayed their decision for a period of time before we have the meeting."

He had taken the risk to call on this new, potentially major customer. The initial response had been negative, but he didn't take that personally; the buyer just didn't understand yet how good a fit our candies would be in her stores! And Keith, most assuredly, was not accepting that no as the final answer.

Intrigued by the situation, I called the buyer myself a few days later. From what she said, I understood that she definitely did not want our chocolates. At that point, I wouldn't have blamed any salesperson for giving up on the account and shifting attention to more receptive customers.

Keith, however, was not just any salesperson. He continued to believe he would eventually get the sale, and he worked gently but persistently toward that end with the buyer. In his mind, the question was not *if* he'd get the sale, but *when*. I quietly shook my head and smiled at his dogged optimism and determination.

Six months later, Keith landed the sale, placing our chocolates in all the chain's stores. The chain became a solid, consistent customer, a steady source of profit for our company.

Effective leaders likewise calculate and accept the risks, don't take the failures personally, and refuse to accept failure as the final answer. Indeed, the failures are often launching points for great learning and subsequent success.

Patience Works

There's a one-word synonym for welcoming small failures: *patience*. In this context, patience means the willingness and ability to endure your own and others' failures because you know that they're inevitable, and that they're such good learning experiences.

Patience is another valuable trait that's usually in short supply but grows naturally out of our cooperating with the work of God's Spirit in our lives. It's a quality he wants to develop in us, a reflection of his own character. Thus, it's something that we can confidently request in prayer, knowing he wants us to have more of it. (But beware: Patience often grows from being put to the test!)

Besides generally needing patience in the face of failure, I've found we also need it in these five specific areas:

1. Making Good Decisions

Almost always, we need to make decisions slowly, after much thought, exploration of alternatives, and prayer. Conversely, the decisions we make in haste are almost always bad ones.

I've made many fast and poor decisions in my career, but one that stands out in my memory was a close call that I made right in the end. It came at a low point in my business life, when I had just taken a huge hit. I was hurting; I was still trying to sort through what had gone wrong and what I should learn from it, and I was feeling alone. To tell the truth, I was wallowing in self-pity.

One day in the midst of that, I got a call from my older son, Brian. Brian and I get along great, and besides that, he's a sharp young man. I'd always thought that if he or my other son or daughter wanted to go into business, they'd be a great success. The idea of working with one of my kids someday had always had great appeal to me. Brian, however, had long dreamed of becoming a doctor, and he was then in his second year of medical school.

As we talked about how things were going, my pain and frustration poured out. Brian listened sympathetically, asked some questions, and tried to understand the situation. I must have sounded pretty low, because after a while he made an extraordinary offer. "Dad, I can tell you aren't your normal self," he said. "Do you want me to come home and work with you?"

Wow, talk about a dream come true! Not only would that have fulfilled my longtime desire, but it also would have made me feel a lot more optimistic about the immediate future of my business. The temptation to shout "Yes!" was incredible. That's certainly what I wanted to do.

I bit my tongue, though, and tried to calm down. My head was swimming; my heart was racing. What might we do together? (I quickly replayed all my daydreams of the two of us building businesses together.) What could I teach him? Speaking of teaching, could he do this and still resume his medical training at some point down the road?

While Brian waited patiently at the other end of the line, I decided to pray. "Lord, I'd love to have him join me," I said silently. "It's been my hope ever since he was born. But as much as I'd like it, is it the right thing in the long run?"

As I thought and prayed along those lines, the realization started to take hold: As much as I wanted to have Brian working with me, the best choice for his future was to stay where he was. His role in life was to heal bodies, not the old man's company.

After a couple of minutes of silent contemplation that seemed to me like an hour, I finally told him, "Thanks for the offer, Brian. I can't tell you how much I appreciate it. And it's mighty tempting. But you need to stay in school and finish the course."

In time, my business bounced back, and Brian got his M.D. Though I continued to imagine what might have been had he come to work with me, the more I thought about it (and discussed it with my wife), the more I knew I had given him the best answer. Jumping on my first choice, the one with the strongest emotional appeal, would have been dead wrong.

2. Getting Staff up to Speed on New Procedures

When you're making changes and trying new things, those small failures are going to happen. But as leaders, while we need to exercise patience with those mistakes, we can also help the staff to learn the lessons as soon as possible and move ahead. How? Not by just holding a meeting and talking about how things ought to be done. Instead, I've found it's invaluable to roll up our sleeves, so to speak, and get in there with the team to work things out.

I recall one occasion when we needed to make a major change in procedures in our shipping department. We had two hundred different products at the time, any or all of which might get packaged and shipped on a given day. So the change would be challenging, even if everything went smoothly. With that complexity, though, and the fact that Murphy's Law has yet to be repealed—not to mention the natural human resistance to change on the part of the crew—implementation was not about to go smoothly.

How might we handle the situation? We could have explained the change, then fussed and fumed and looked for someone to blame when problems developed. But instead, I dedicated the next two days of my time to working in the shipping department, side by side with the regular team.

I showed them what we had in mind and why we thought it would improve things. When the inevitable glitches arose, we looked at what had gone wrong and adjusted the procedure accordingly. When someone had a question, we found the answer together. The team saw that senior staff respected their work, understood their concerns, had reasonable expectations, and was dedicated to their success.

Within a couple of weeks, the new procedure was indeed saving us money and helping shipping to run more smoothly.

3. Negotiating Deals

Working out the terms of a contract is supposed to be a win-win proposition where each side gets what it needs and at least some of what it wants. When a deal looks great and you're anxious to close, however, you can quickly lose patience and rush into an agreement that you'll soon regret.

If you're smart, you'll need to be taught this painful lesson only once or twice. Thereafter, *patience* and *due diligence* will become the words by which you live.

At a certain point, when the chocolate business was going great, we had some profits to put to work, and I had the entrepreneurial itch to find some good, new deals. I had always wanted to start a restaurant chain, so my team and I did research on what opportunities were available in our area.

We found a steak house for sale close by that was part of a chain; it had prospered in the 1970s but struggled in the '80s. Now it appeared to be on the comeback trail. We bought the restaurant and went to work.

As the first months passed, business was okay but not great. We were learning as we went, trying different promotions and menu items that sometimes worked and sometimes didn't. On the whole, we were optimistic about the future, but it was still early in the game.

Then one day we got a call from the chain's corporate office. Would we be interested in buying a few more restaurants? I felt I had the time to devote to the project. I was eager to build my chain. A few months as a restaurateur had me thinking I knew the business inside out and could handle whatever challenges came along. I jumped at the offer, and we bought three more restaurants.

Well, as the saying goes, they saw us coming. The problems with these stores were more serious than we had understood—a fact we likely would have discovered had we investigated more carefully. And to our dismay, the things we'd learned from running the one restaurant for a limited time had not prepared us to resolve these issues. For the next two years, we literally paid the price for my haste. Every profit and loss statement showed how much we'd lost in the month just past and reinforced my expensive lesson in deal making.

4. Developing Your Own Skills

As leaders, we need to be developing our own skills constantly. Much as we'd like to master new abilities immediately, we're going to stumble along the way. These also are learning opportunities, and patience is again vital.

One important leadership skill is proficiency in reading people, in seeing past the hype and the good front that many folks are able to put on. This in itself requires patience, because it's easy to get caught up in the excitement that others generate. This is another lesson I've had to learn the hard way.

During one period of my entrepreneurial life, my son David and I were running a consulting business together. We had just lost out on a fairly large contract, so we were hungry for a promising deal. Then along came the flamboyant owner of a shipping company, wanting our help. Bobby was a one-man show, a terrific guy who never met a stranger, as the saying goes. At one trade show we attended with him, people lined up to shake his hand and talk or share a joke with him.

His business was ready to explode, Bobby said. Potential customers were calling him all the time. If we could help him streamline his expenses and develop a better integrated computer system for keeping track of everything, he'd be able to handle a lot more shipments, and we'd get a slice of the profits.

Bobby's charisma and sales pitch won us over. Without researching his industry in general, or his company in particular, we jumped on board—no money in hand but the promise of big things to come.

You can guess what happened. We did our part. Over the next six months, we got his firm in position to handle a flood of new business, and then we waited . . . and waited . . . and waited. The reality began to sink in that the torrent existed only in Bobby's imagination. If we wanted to see any payoff from all our efforts, we were also going to have to go out and drum up new sales for him. Our "sure thing" had turned into a tough hill to climb, with very iffy prospects.

5. Looking within When Things Go Wrong

Finally, when the failures come along, large or small, our natural human tendency is to look "outside" for the cause, to affix blame as quickly as possible on someone or something. But leaders who want both real and lasting success develop the patience and wisdom to look within themselves first for the core problem. They won't always find it there, but many times they will.

This is tough, because we want to deny the truth of our own shortcomings. I've been as guilty of this as anyone.

Andrew ran one of our restaurants. He was smart, friendly, and just generally a good person. Everyone in our company liked working with him. Unfortunately, he wasn't a good restaurant manager. He couldn't keep his food or labor costs under control, and that's a surefire recipe for disaster. Month by month, the cash flow from his store was dropping.

My team and I knew the restaurant was in trouble. We also knew that the only way to turn things around was to replace Andrew. But because we liked him, we didn't want to do that. So we kept him on, and the cash flow kept sinking.

To justify that nondecision to ourselves, we told one another that the cost of food just kept increasing, ignoring Andrew's poor control of portions and waste. We remarked that good help is hard to find, overlooking all the overtime he was paying. This went on for the better part of a year, by the end of which we were almost in a position of having to shut down the restaurant.

Fortunately, that prospect finally brought us to our senses. We asked ourselves, Have we been jumping to the easy, comfortable answers as to what's wrong with that store? Is the root problem really "out there," or is it within us? Have we known all along what needed to happen but been unwilling to do it?

Examined in that cold light of reality, the answers were clear. We let Andrew go, painful as it was to do so, and began to turn the business around.

In any enterprise, small failures are inevitable. We can try to deny that fact and be constantly frustrated, or we can welcome them as learning opportunities. Since we can't avoid the pain, let's make the most of it. Let's cash in on it. Then, when it's gone, we'll be smarter for it and won't have wasted it.

Can You Taste Success?

1. What has been your perspective on "small failures" in the past? How has it changed as a result of reading this chapter?
2. I've defined failure as not even trying something new and promising because of fear. How willing are you to take such risks? Why?
3. How do you tend to deal with rejection of your ideas or proposals? How might that need to change?
4. In which of the five areas in which patience is needed do you most need to grow? Why?
5. When things do go wrong, is your first impulse to blame the circumstances, blame someone else, or blame yourself? How does each of these affect your ability to learn from the experience?

PURSUE NEW IDEAS, NO MATTER HOW HEAVY THE CURRENT DEMANDS

When you're in the habit of always being on the lookout for new ideas, you never know where they're going to pop up. A walk in some thick, darkened woods once inspired an idea for a Black Forest truffle. However, the strong flavor of dark chocolate overpowered the sweetness of the cherries. The candy maker realized that just as sunlight breaking through the trees added to the woods' beauty, a little cherry flavoring in addition to the fruit itself could make a tastier truffle.

Winning leaders know the Black Forest truffle principle: You'll always find great ideas where you least expect them, and when you start looking for them, your organization will really go places.

Normally, I'm very aware of the need to be open to new ideas, to look for major trends, and to get a jump start on new products that will meet new demands. Normally.

In the early 1980s, sugar-free foods started to appear in the market. Doing our job as leaders, my senior management team and I looked into whether we should develop a line of sugar-free chocolates. We found that this appeared to be a trend with legs: About 10 to 12 percent of the market wanted sugar-free foods because people were hypoglycemic, diabetic, or allergic to sugar; they just thought sugar-free was better for them; or it would help them lose weight.

So far, so good. But there were problems.

For one thing, the FDA would allow food makers to use only certain sugar substitutes. For another, all the allowable substitutes lost their potency, their sweetness, when heated above certain temperatures. And the capper? To be used in our chocolates, they all had to be cooked above the "safe" temperatures.

The result was that, in my opinion, there was simply no way to make an acceptable-tasting sugar-free chocolate. The flavor just wasn't up to our usual standards. So I concluded that we should not move ahead with a sugar-free product, as doing so could only damage our reputation. Being known for producing only premium-tasting candies was more important, I was sure, than having a sugar-free line in our catalog.

At the same time, some of our competitors came to the opposite conclusion. They decided that the demand for sugar-free was so great that they should meet it, even if the taste quality suffered.

In retrospect, our competitors were obviously right. Enough people wanted sugar-free, regardless of the compromise in flavor, that it became a huge market.

Belatedly, still reluctantly, I gave in and agreed that we should put our own sugar-free chocolates into production. But even once we had them, we had trouble getting them into the market. Customers who might have bought sugar-free from us in the past were already buying it from our competitors. Thus, getting our sugar-free product into stores proved to be a slow and difficult process.

The bottom line: We were two years late getting our chocolates established in the market, and we never did gain as big a share of the sugar-free market as we might have, had we jumped into the front end of the trend instead of crawling in at the back.

As I've said before, and as you, no doubt, experience every day, modern leaders face heavy, often crushing, demands. Just staying on top of supply issues, personnel issues, accounting issues, manufacturing problems, and the like is more than a full-time job. Many of us work well beyond the forty-hour week merely to keep current projects and programs going.

Busy as we already are, however, we simply can't neglect the pursuit of new ideas. Today's new ideas are tomorrow's programs and products. Those, in turn, will be a crucial part of the organization's ongoing income and profits. The world in general, and business in particular, never stands still, and it is the same with individual companies. You're either moving forward or falling behind.

The opening story is a good illustration of how the world and markets change. Sometimes the changes are dramatic, and other times they're small, but the only constant in life is that things *will* change. If you don't make the right adjustments, one or more of your competitors will.

Thus, making the time to pursue new ideas—to find them, test them, and develop the most promising ones—cannot be an afterthought for successful leaders.

It can't be something we put just a few minutes into if there's any time left at the end of the day, when we've checked off everything else on the to-do list.

It can't be "just a nice concept," for which we really don't have time.

Instead, we have to see it as one of the most vital parts of our work.

Admit You Don't Know It All

One of the keys to pursuing new ideas is simply to recognize that there's a lot you don't know. For myself, that recognition keeps me humble enough to learn and hungry enough for knowledge that I always want to learn more. It also keeps my mind open to new ideas, because I'm confident they're out there, just waiting to be discovered. And God's Spirit gives me joy in the search; it's truly one of the most enjoyable parts of my work.

Where do we find these ideas? In books, newsletters, magazines, and on the Internet, for starters. This is why it's so necessary that a leader be a reader. Seminars and conferences are another good source, as are industry-related conventions. (It's amazing how much you can learn just by walking around and seeing what others are doing.) And naturally, you should talk with others in your field and in related areas.

Of course, an overabundance of information is available these days, so sorting through it all becomes a challenge. One way to do that is to seek recommendations from people whose judgment you trust. We all rely on favorite magazines, books, and web sites.

Another way I sort through the piles of information, as I have mentioned, is to categorize the material that's worth keeping as either "need to know" or "good to know." The material that's "need to know"—that has immediate or obviously vital future application to my work—I put at the top of my list and get to as soon as possible, in one of the regular times I set aside every week for reading and research.

The "good to know" material, on the other hand, I put lower on my list. I aim to get through it all eventually, though it may take a while. At least once a week, I skim through my stack to make sure that everything there still merits at least a "good to know" rating. Anything that doesn't, I toss.

Another key is, whenever possible, to have a defined target in the search for new ideas. If I'm looking for an idea to help with a particular need, for example, my pursuit can be much more focused. Let me illustrate what I mean.

In my wife's cooking school, we had been thinking for some time about offering a program for people who were seriously interested in becoming chefs but who had full-time jobs and couldn't afford to become full-time students. We had kicked around lots of ideas about class structure and size, who the instructors might be, and so on. But we felt as if we were going around in circles, not really progressing toward viable, firm plans.

Then we took a trip to another state and spent some time with a company that already had such a program up and running. Its administrators had already wrestled with the same questions we faced and found answers. Based on their experience, they could tell us that some approaches just wouldn't work but that options C and D were both feasible, and so on.

With those insights, suddenly we could focus our thinking and our search for ideas. Some of our questions had been answered; we could concentrate on the ones that remained. Instead of sorting through five options in a given area, we could decide which of only two best fit our situation. Our targets were much better defined and, therefore, easier to hit.

Yet another key in the search for new ideas is to have a hunger for excellence. To be in a position of leadership is both a great privilege and a great responsibility. Employees and their families, suppliers and their families, customers, and many others are counting on you to do your job well. I, for one, take that calling seriously and want not just to muddle through, but to excel in my work. Since I know that pursuing new ideas is an indispensable part of that job, and I draw strength and self-discipline from God's Spirit, I'm motivated and enabled to give it my best effort.

Leader, Beware

Through experiences, often painful, I've also learned that you have to watch out for certain red flags as you pursue new ideas. Here are the five biggest:

1. Easy Ideas

If anyone says developing a new product will be effortless, a new program will be simple to implement, or there's an easy way to do some job, *run*. Don't even take time to listen. Things are always harder, more complicated, and time consuming (and expensive), than you expect. I'm not sure why that's true, but it is—invariably.

2. Too Much Change at Once

In our chocolate company, the rule was that we wouldn't change more than 10 percent of our product line in any one year. If we tried to change more, both quality and customer loyalty were likely to suffer—the latter because people seem to assume that since we were changing so much, our company must be in trouble and getting desperate.

This is yet another lesson I learned the hard way. One year, when our sales were flat, ecology emerged as a prominent issue. Green was in; "Save the rain forests" became the hot new motto. In our senior staff meetings, we discussed ways that we might plug in to this trend.

We decided that, especially in light of the need to jump-start our sales, we should give it a go.

We came up with a couple of new box designs that featured a tropical look, with many pastel colors. The materials were completely recyclable. We planned to donate some of the proceeds to a "save the rain forests" fund, and we had that fact printed on the boxes.

The more we worked on the project, the more excited and hopeful we grew. We were sure we had a big-time winner on our hands. Soon we had a whole new line featuring *six* different boxes, not just one or two new boxes added to our existing line, and our runaway enthusiasm had flattened the 10 percent rule.

Well, to put it mildly, the new line proved to be a complete flop. The store buyers to whom we sold never shared our excitement. The product that did make it onto retail shelves just sat there, as consumers weren't drawn to it either. In my mind's eye, I can still see all those pallets of beautiful boxes stacked in our warehouse—boxes we had been sure we'd need when the product started flying off the shelves, boxes for which we had absolutely no use when the line bombed.

Our losses on this experiment set us back big-time financially. We shook our heads and renewed our commitment to the 10 percent rule.

3. Decisions Made in Isolation

You need help. Once you have an idea that you feel good about, run it by *all* your senior staff. They can assist you by refining the idea and by catching things you may have overlooked.

Here's an example. We came up with an idea for a foot-long, half-inch-thick pretzel to be dipped in chocolate and called the Texas Toothpick. We put it in a clear package, and it had great eye appeal. At the candy shows where we displayed prototypes, people loved it, and our sales staff wrote lots of orders.

Based on that response, we invested a lot of time and money in retooling the production line, laying in inventory, buying the packaging, making marketing plans, and so on.

What we didn't do was check with our shipping department about how such a product would likely fare in the rough-and-tumble world of package delivery. So, what we discovered the hard way was that the answer to the unasked question was "Badly." It seemed that as many Texas Toothpicks arrived at the stores broken as arrived safely.

Belatedly, we implored the shipping folks to try to find a way to deliver them in one piece. Unfortunately, every way was prohibitively expensive.

The net result was that we made no money from Texas Toothpicks, and clearly we never would. Before long, we had to admit our mistake and pull the product from our line.

4. Naysayers

Some will always object to anything that's new and different. "We've never done something like that before" is their mantra. "We don't know how to market it," they'll add. "We don't know how to project sales."

Of course, you need to heed legitimate concerns, such as when your shipping experts tell you there's no way to get the product delivered in one piece. But don't let naysayers kill an idea before you even have a chance to fully explore it. Listen to their concerns attentively and with respect, and use them to sharpen your idea. But don't be hasty in abandoning any promising idea, just as you shouldn't be hasty in developing any idea when a staff member has pointed out legitimate flaws in it.

5. Assigning Roles in One Big Meeting

If you take the usual approach, which is to hold a single launch meeting in which everyone receives his or her assignment at the same time, here's what's likely to happen:

You wanted Joe in inventory control to make sure that enough of the newly designed boxes would be on hand for the launch of the new campaign. Joe somehow got the impression in the meeting, however, that that responsibility fell to Jane in purchasing. For her part, Jane better understood your instructions and left the meeting confident that Joe was going to take care of ensuring an adequate supply of boxes.

Several months go by. You're sure Joe is arranging for the new boxes. Jane is sure of the same thing. Joe has the same feeling of certainty that Jane is getting the boxes.

Now the day of the big launch is fast approaching. You convene another all-hands meeting to double-check that the many pieces for the campaign are coming together as planned.

Yes, you hear, the new product is turning out well and has begun rolling off the line.

Yes, the marketing materials look good; staffers have sent them out, and they've purchased ad space timed to coincide with the official release date of the new product.

Yes, the sales staff has been getting a positive response from core customers. Your vice president of sales says it looks as though profits will soon be rocketing through the roof. He's sure glad everything is on track to ship the product according to schedule.

Turning to Joe, you say, "Oh, that's your cue, Joe. Since we haven't heard of any red flags, we assume the new boxes are in the warehouse, or will be very soon. Right?"

Joe, smiling at your "misstatement," looks at Jane and says with a chuckle, "You meant to ask Jane that, didn't you?"

Jane, her smile suddenly turning into a quizzical look and then a worried frown, responds, "What are you talking about, Joe?"

Finally, over the next ten minutes, as the crossed wires of communication are at last laid bare, the feeling of elation in the room turns to consternation and then panic. Everything else will be ready for the launch, but there will be no boxes.

Actually, if only one big thing like that went wrong in launching a new campaign, you'd be doing better than average.

Now, think how much better that scenario would have gone if you had met with each key player and handed out assignments individually. You would have looked Joe in the eye and told him, "Joe, it's your job to make sure those new boxes are here in time for the campaign launch. Get Jane in purchasing and Carl in shipping to help if you need it, but the responsibility is yours. The buck stops with you. As we track our progress in preparing for this launch, I'll be asking *you* about the boxes. Any questions?"

No one else would have been in the room. Joe would have had no doubt that the job was his.

New ideas, which lead to new products and services and improved ways of doing the old, are the lifeblood of any organization. Finding them and nurturing them is a crucial part of the work of every leader, whether or not it's written into the job description.

Pursue those ideas vigorously. Put that pursuit at or near the top of your priority list, not the bottom. The fate of your enterprise depends upon it.

Can You Taste Success?

1. How high a priority have you been placing on seeking out new ideas? When can you carve out time for it each week?
2. Whose recommendations do you or could you trust for good sources of new ideas?
3. How might you better define your target in your search for ideas? For what kinds of ideas, or in which areas, do you have the greatest need?
4. What kinds of limits does your organization have on changing too much at one time? What limits might it need?
5. What obstacles do you face in trying to implement new ideas? How can you work to overcome them?

173

LET PASSION FUEL YOUR WORK

The same chemical that stimulates your taste buds when you eat chocolate (phenylethylamine) stirs the brain when you're in love.
In the same way that chocolate nurtures its own passion, a winning leader loves his or her purpose so much that it can create a craving in others to be a part of the mission or business.

It may surprise you to learn that when I bought my chocolate company, I knew nothing more about chocolate than the average person. Nor was I particularly passionate about chocolate. Oh, I liked it well enough, but by no means was I one of the millions of fanatics who claim that chocolate is one of the major food groups and that their health will suffer if they don't have five servings a day!

The simple fact is that I bought the company, not out of a love for chocolate, but because I saw it as a good business deal and an incredible project.

As surprising as this news might be to you, it would be downright shocking to employees who joined the company, say, six or twelve months into its new life. By then I practically lived and breathed chocolate, and many employees were fond of saying that I had chocolate running through my veins!

This transformation developed over time and out of necessity. To run the company well, I realized I had to know my product. I had to learn about different kinds and grades of chocolate, not to mention all the other ingredients that go into fine candies. Basically, I needed to discover the difference between the everyday candy bar and top-quality, exquisite chocolates.

Knowing what I didn't know, I set about gaining the requisite understanding. I read books and articles—everything I could get my hands on. I attended seminars and conferences. I crammed my mind with facts about chocolate and how it's made, from growing the bean on the tree in Costa Rica to getting the box on the shelf of a candy shop in mid-America.

As I learned, I grew fascinated. A great piece of chocolate is truly a work of art, combining the finest ingredients with careful attention to cooking and preparation. Lesser-quality ingredients and shortcuts in manufacture are possible—lots of companies use them every day—but not if you want to be able to make the case that your chocolates are among the best that can be had at any price.

With my respect and admiration for good chocolate increasing, I told everyone what I was learning—constantly. I kept a mug on my desk that said, "If you find me listless and depressed, administer chocolate immediately." I just couldn't stop talking about it! You might say I became a passionate proselytizer for chocolate.

Then, to my surprise, my love for chocolate grew contagious. A real corporate craze for it developed. We truly came to care about making great chocolate, not just pushing a product out the door.

Knowing we were committed to making the finest chocolates, we in the leadership team also told everyone in the company, "We have the opportunity to make people happy by giving them a great-looking and great-tasting box of chocolates! What better way to make a living than to make people happy for a while?"

Since most everyone likes to make others happy, that proved to be a good motivator. Between that desire and our passion for chocolate, we soon had a team of people who loved what they were doing and why they were doing it. And for a leader, life doesn't get much better than that.

Gaining and maintaining a passion for your work isn't just a good idea. It's absolutely essential to successful leadership.

This also represents a major change in my thinking. I used to believe that all I needed to do was work hard, give clear instructions to staff, and pay people fairly. As long as they knew what I expected and got a paycheck every Friday, what more could they require of a leader?

Experience has taught me, however, that passion is also required. If you don't keep a fire going internally, you won't survive, and your people won't be inspired, either. Let me explain.

I've talked before about how tough leadership is. You work long hours, probably longer than anyone else on the team. You don't relax enough, sleep enough, or spend as much time with your family as you'd like. You push yourself hard day after day. If you're like many, you load up with caffeine to keep yourself going when your energy flags.

Even when you're not in the office, your work is often on your mind. If you're anything like me, when there are any problems or challenges in the business (which is to say, just about every day), they prey on your mind and make sleep difficult.

You're dealing with supply problems, cash flow problems, personnel problems, quality control problems, unhappy customer problems, and so on. To paraphrase the old spiritual, "Nobody knows the trouble you've seen."

It's nice if you're paid well, but that means nothing when you're under the gun in the midst of a battle for your firm's future—or even worse, a battle for corporate survival. And if you're an entrepreneur and it's *your* small business, the financial reward may not even be there. You may be pouring almost everything you make back into the business to pay the rent, build inventory, or meet payroll.

In the face of all that, what's going to keep you pushing ahead? What's going to stop you from running up the white flag of surrender and walking away?

The answer is *passion*. Love for the company. Love for the product or service you provide, and for knowing how it enhances the lives of your customers. Love for your teammates.

On good days and bad—but especially on the bad—you had better have a fire in your gut for the work you're doing or it will be hard to stay in the struggle. Hanging in there and dealing with all the hassles just won't be worth the price, no matter how well you're paid.

As I mentioned, your passion is also vital to your people. The biggest impact you have as a leader is in the example you set. If you're not passionate about what you're doing, if you're just showing up to collect a check, the staff around you will quickly pick up on that, and your attitude will become their attitude. Then, no matter what you say or what motivational techniques you might try, you won't be able to make them care about their work.

The good news, though, is that the flip side of the coin is also true. When you *are* passionate about what you're doing—when you live and breathe and talk about it all the time—your coworkers will pick up on that and soon make your passion their own.

I enjoyed experiencing that when I became passionate about chocolate and about making our customers happy by supplying them with great candies. My teammates caught my passion and soon shared it. Before long, we were all excited about making superb chocolates, putting them in beautiful packages, and knowing we were brightening the day of everyone who took home one of our boxes.

Passion Overcomes Tedium

Passion also makes the difference when your work requires you to do something that goes against your grain. For example, I'm a big-picture kind of person. I like to come up with new ideas, lay broad plans, pull together the people and resources, and then let others work out and administer the details.

When you run a company, a *lot* of details demand your attention. Some you can (and *should*) delegate to others. But some you can't avoid if you're going to do your job properly. And in the chocolate company, one of the things I had to be involved with every year was the pricing of our products. Talk about tedious! I *hated* doing it. But I had to make the final call.

Pricing products is always a tough challenge. On the one hand, you'd like to charge as much as you can so as to make the biggest possible profit. On the other hand, you know that at some point, customers will stop buying and turn to your competitors. You also have to estimate what all your costs will be going forward—labor, utilities, chocolate and sugar and every other ingredient, and so on—and set your prices high enough to cover all those expenses, plus provide a profit.

If you underestimate any of your costs for any reason, or you overestimate how popular one or more of your products will be, your profits can disappear in a hurry. So every year, after all my staff members had done their best to project every expense and the sale of every product, and the accounting people had crunched the numbers to come up with appropriate prices, I gritted my teeth and worked through every line of that report.

This was several days' work and pure torture, as far as I was concerned. Do you realize that some chocolate candies have as many as nine ingredients, and an administrator has to consider the projected cost of each in pricing the one item? That's a lot of detail for a big-picture person!

It's not that I didn't trust my people. It's just that the product pricing was so important that I considered it my duty to make sure it was done properly and to take the responsibility for the final decisions.

Believe me, if I hadn't been passionate about my work, I would have found some excuse to wiggle out of that job.

Regaining Lost Passion

As important as it is, passion for your work—because it has a large emotional component—can weaken at times. Fatigue, fear, and other interests can cause it to fade. When you realize that's happening, what can you do to recover your love? Through my own ups and downs, I've discovered two remedies that help get me back on track.

First and most important, you can pray that God will restore your passion and give you wisdom in dealing with whatever problem caused it to dim.

I recall a time when our cash flow was extremely low, leading us to consider desperate measures. Should we cut staff? Should we put off developing new products in order to postpone the expenses? Could we cut costs in any other ways, seeing that all our efforts to increase income seemed to be going nowhere?

Wrestling emotionally and mentally with these tough issues and decisions kept me from sleeping well. I lived and worked in a constant fog of sleep deprivation. Fear about what might happen also gnawed at the back of my mind constantly—and often at the front as well! Once again, the final call for choices that would affect many lives landed squarely on my shoulders.

I was definitely not loving my work.

Finally one evening, in the middle of another sleepless night, the anxiety and indecision overwhelmed me so completely that I felt as if I were going to be swallowed alive! Almost in a panic, I climbed out of bed, walked down to my home office, and got on my knees. Then I laid before God every concern and every option under consideration for dealing with the situation.

I didn't hear any audible voices from heaven or get any brilliant flashes of insight that night. But here's what did happen: Starting that evening, and growing in the following days as I continued to pray, I gradually gained a renewed sense that God was in charge and I didn't need to fear. I also began to see new possibilities for addressing the problems. And along with these came a reinvigorating of my passion.

One of the ideas that came to me in this time of prayer and study was to keep all our employees but cut their workweek from five days to four (a decision I discussed in an earlier chapter). This enabled our people to keep their jobs and paychecks while we cut our costs substantially.

Putting the decision into practice wasn't easy for any-one, because those paychecks were suddenly smaller. Obviously, it wasn't an ideal solution, but it seemed to be the best alternative. The staff and their families were able to keep going, and so was our chocolate company. My own growing optimism and confidence that God was in the decision fueled optimism and confidence in the crew as well.

Eventually, our sales and cash flow started to improve. When the pace of business appeared strong enough and sustainable, we gladly put everyone back on a five-day schedule.

Rekindling the Satisfaction of Success

Another way to regain lost passion is to take small steps and build on small victories. It's like the old clichéd question and answer: How do you eat an elephant? You can't possibly tackle it all at once or swallow it whole. So you do it one bite at a time.

At one point, my son and I went to work with a person who had a great idea for a restaurant concept. Based on our experience in that field, we believed it could be a huge success. So for two years, we worked long and hard to get the restaurant up and running. We even did

184

it for little pay, with the understanding that we would get a healthy share of the profits when they started appearing.

Over the course of those two years, we developed a real passion for the project. We anticipated serving lots of good food, in a fun atmosphere, to satisfied customers. As with the chocolate company, I was thinking, *What better way to make a living than to make people happy for a while?*

Just as we were getting the business off to a strong start, however, the deal went south. Our partner, the guy who had the original concept, announced that he felt he should get a larger share of the coming profits. My son and I considered the existing arrangement to be fair, and we tried to reason with the man. We had invested so much time, energy, and passion, we really wanted to work things out.

Our partner dug in his heels, though, and refused to budge. The terms he demanded were so unfavorable to us that we saw we would actually lose money if we agreed to them. In the end, despite our best efforts to reach a compromise, we had to give up and walk away from the project.

The experience left me totally deflated. I was physically and emotionally exhausted. With no other job prospects at hand, I also faced an uncertain, fearful future.

How could I regain some passion and get back on my feet? The temptation was to look for another big deal, the kind of thing I had worked up to over the years—a deal that would generate a lot of income right off the bat.

Try as I might, however, I couldn't get anything to work. I didn't realize, at the time, how much the busted partnership had hurt my confidence, or how that lack of confidence was undermining my efforts. After a few months of going nowhere, I took stock of the situation and decided I had better try another approach.

My son and I assessed the market and the limited resources we had to work with and then decided to open a deli. Making take-out sandwiches for the lunch crowd was a far cry from the grand restaurant scheme we had been honing previously! The hours were many, the work grueling. The cash flow was much smaller than we had grown accustomed to seeing.

In a nutshell, we found nothing glamorous or exciting about running a neighborhood deli.

Gradually, though, the business came alive. First, a few people became aware of us and tried us out. Then we ran some promotions, and more people responded. That gave us a glimmer of hope. Next, because we offered good sandwiches at fair prices, we started to see repeat customers—the lifeblood of any successful enterprise.

These small steps, producing small victories, steadily recharged my battery and restored my confidence. We expanded our menu, and people liked the new items. We advertised more, and sales grew. This was like Business 101, about as basic as you can get—and it proved to be exactly what I needed.

It's amazing the difference a healthy mind-set can make. As the deli business was growing, I was also trying to run a business brokerage on the side (being an agent who helps clients buy and sell businesses). For more than a year, as my passion and confidence continued to wane, I didn't sell a thing.

Then, as the deli began to prosper and my passion rekindled, I sold my first business through the brokerage. No big change had occurred in the local economy, in interest rates, or in any other external factor. The only major change had taken place inside *me*.

That success so pumped up my confidence and increased my passion that I made yet another sale just a couple of months later. Before long, as a result of having taken small steps with the deli and building on the small victories, I was again enjoying the satisfaction of success.

But Heed the Red Flags

Having addressed the importance of passion and how to regain it when you've lost it, I now need to point out that you should keep certain cautions in mind. In particular, I've seen a couple of potentially serious problems related to passion.

Remember to Serve

First, as leaders, we must never forget that our work is all about serving others. We're providing a product or service that we live and breathe, whether it's chocolate or something else. In doing so, we meet the needs of customers and provide jobs for our employees. All that is worth getting excited about, wouldn't you agree?

When we forget that we're supposed to be servants, however—when we start to think that we're the center of our world, when ego and ambition and a self-serving attitude take over—both we and those around us will see our passion drain away quickly. It's a cliché but it's true: The more you give, the more you get. And conversely, the more you try to grab, the less you'll actually have.

As another true cliché says, people will run through a brick wall for someone who clearly has their best interests at heart. But they'll give minimal effort, at best, for someone who's pursuing his own selfish interests at their expense.

How do we maintain a servant's heart? For me, the key is to spend at least thirty minutes at the beginning of the day in prayer and in reading the Bible. Those things remind me that God and his plans are a lot bigger than me and mine, and that there are eternal principles and values that ought to guide my conduct.

When I fail to have that "quiet time" on a given day—and especially if I neglect to do it for several days, or even a week or more—I soon start to feel the impact. My energy drops. My passion fades. Challenges start to seem overwhelming. My temper gets short. And I notice that other people begin to take notice!

If you, like me, sometimes start to lose a healthy perspective, make that daily time for your own attitude adjustment. And it wouldn't hurt, either, to give your spouse or a trusted friend permission to let you know, gently, when such an adjustment is overdue.

Remember to Blend Passion with Wisdom

The second caution is that when you're passionate about what you're doing, and you're working hard, it's easy to think that focused labor is all that really matters. But that's simply not the case. *The world doesn't pay for effort; it pays for results.*

As the pioneering carmaker Henry Ford pointed out, the farmer wants to be paid as much for his work as an industrialist like Ford. The farmer claims to work harder, and he's probably right. But the world doesn't pay for sweat. It pays for outcome.

Thus, passion alone is not enough. It has to be tempered with wisdom.

Let me give you an example. I've written in earlier chapters about the dangers of debt. Well, when you're passionate about your work—your product, your company—and business is going poorly, the fast and simple fix is to borrow money. It's easy, caught up in the emotion, for any company head to rationalize and justify the decision. What should be the last resort then becomes the first resort. What should be primarily a means of fueling growth in a healthy enterprise becomes, instead, a means of trying to keep a struggling enterprise afloat.

What's the one thing that's true of every company that ends up having to declare bankruptcy? Its debts are larger than its assets!

We should think of debt like dynamite: Used carefully and properly, it has great power to do useful work. But used unwisely and improperly, it can and will destroy.

Passion alone is not enough. Passion *with wisdom* is a winning combination.

I recall, all too well, a number of occasions when passion led me down an unwise path. There was the time, for instance, when our office expenses seemed out of control in the chocolate company. My response was to become a passionate cost cutter, a fanatic for frugality.

Now, to my credit, I set an example in such things as turning out unneeded lights. People followed my lead pretty well. But then, looking for further savings, I insisted that all the employees start keeping track of how many copies they made on the Xerox machine.

That was a step too far. It turned the good general principle of keeping an eye on expenses into a major annoyance. After my announcement, I heard some folks grumble. I saw others engage in passive aggression, saying nothing but simply refusing to comply.

After a couple of days of this, with the office atmosphere having turned noticeably sour, I realized my passion had run amok. I decided to drop the policy and admit to everyone that I had overdone it.

On another occasion, passion led me to push a new product too hard too fast. As a small company looking for a product that would help us to stand out in the marketplace, we hit on the idea of trying to offer a lower-fat nut candy. People love chocolate-covered peanuts, but peanuts are high in fat.

A cottonseed company had approached us. "Cottonseeds are lower in fat than peanuts," they said, "yet people tell us they taste a lot alike." So we developed a nut cluster with cottonseeds dipped in white chocolate.

Sure enough, our taste testers told us the flavor was quite similar to that of a peanut cluster. We had the best of both worlds: a popular taste but a lower fat content. We introduced it to the market and received a strong response. Encouraged and excited, we pushed even harder.

Sales took off. Our excitement turned to passion. We had something new that we had thought of first! We *loved* this product. It was going to put us on the map. To paraphrase a popular song from the 1970s, "the future suddenly seemed so bright that we had to wear shades!" We started to dream big dreams and spin big plans.

Then came the call from one of our retailers in El Paso, Texas. Seems that a customer had sampled one of our cottonseed clusters at the candy counter and immediately gone into shock! The store manager had called an ambulance, which transported the person to the hospital.

The problem, as it turned out, was pretty simple. Just as some folks are allergic to peanuts, some—usually the same people—are allergic to cottonseeds. But because we had been so passionate and excited about the new product, we hadn't taken the time and effort to test whether anyone might have such a reaction to it. Frankly, we hadn't even paused to consider the possibility.

As I indicated earlier, fear is one of the things that can kill passion, and after that incident I was terrified! Visions of costly allergy studies and lawsuits suddenly danced in my head, supplanting all those big dreams. For a small company like ours, expensive tests and legal action could spell disaster.

I felt as if someone had snuck up and popped our beautiful balloon. We just dropped the new product and walked away, vowing never to let ourselves be so overcome by passion again.

Passion. Love for your work. It's essential. If you lose it, you'd better find it again as quickly as possible. Always temper it with wisdom, of course, because it has the power to mislead badly, with potentially devastating consequences. But if you maintain a healthy perspective and keep it under control, it will not only fuel your success as a leader, but it will also make every day a lot more fun!

Can You Taste Success?

1. On a scale from one (couldn't care less) to ten (couldn't love it more), how passionate do you feel about your work at the present time? Why?
2. What are some parts of your job that you really don't enjoy? How might passion help you get through them?
3. What aspects of your situation right now—fear, fatigue, or some other interest—might be draining away your passion for your work?
4. If you lack passion for your work, or you had it before but now have lost it, what steps can you take, beginning today, to start or restart the fire in your belly?
5. Think of a time when passion for some part of the work led you or a coworker to take unwise action. What lessons can you learn from that experience to help you better handle the next time passion threatens to mislead you?

EMBRACE THE POWER OF HUMILITY

The many people who contribute to making a great line of chocolates never see their names printed on the box. Yet they are essential ingredients for this fickle food that melts at 80 degrees and must be meticulously tended and nurtured without additives for the best taste.

So it is with a great leader: Working in essential ways, behind the scenes and with little acclaim, winning leaders attentively nurture a business so that everyone, from customers to the corporate janitor, tastes sweet success.

One December evening my staff and I, along with assorted family members, were enjoying the annual company Christmas party. Everyone was having a good time with the fellowship, the food, and the fun of a carol sing-along—and, of course, chocolate! Then came the time for the gag gift exchange.

Everything went about as you'd expect until one guy opened his present and discovered that he had received a yo-yo. Now, many of the party goers were men, and I think the sight of that yo-yo brought back memories of childhood exploits for us all. When the exchange was completed, we all gathered around the guy with the yo-yo, wanting a turn to show what we could do.

Soon the testosterone-laced competition was in full roar. I noticed that a few guys, apparently afraid of being embarrassed, hung back, content to watch. *Poor them, I* thought. *They should be in control and fearless like me!*

I waited impatiently for my chance. In my day I had swung a pretty mean yo-yo. Finally my turn came. I—the boss, the CEO, the buck-stops-here guy—would now put on a jaw-dropping demonstration of yo-yo skill.

As I stood in the middle of the group and slid the slip-knotted loop over my finger, I thought of my glory days with the yo-yo. Then my mind flashed to days ahead when I envisioned myself at the office water cooler, where employees would recount the events of this party, saying things like "Did you see Bill with that yo-yo? He was incredible!"

I announced that I would perform the famous "rock the baby" trick—my specialty! I thought, *Not many people can do this maneuver as well as I can!* It never occurred to me that my skills might have diminished some over the years from lack of practice.

The trick went great . . . for the first millisecond. Then, as the "baby" swung over the top, instead of falling neatly into the rocking position, things went terribly wrong. Now feeling like a two-ton rock, the yo-yo headed straight for my crotch and scored a direct, full-throttle hit!

As I bent over in agony, my confident, proud demeanor was instantly replaced with a look of pain and shock. Glancing up, I saw that my audience first seemed horrified and then broke out into uncontrollable laughter. I couldn't blame them, I guess. So much for glory days.

As I'd predicted, my yo-yo demonstration became a hot topic for water cooler conversations, and it remained so for weeks to come. In fact, I suppose my coworkers still bring it up every now and then as they pack the chocolates and wrap those boxes.

Of course, the incident did not become famous for the reason I had expected and hoped. But it surely popped my balloon of pride, which was a good thing. And indeed even now, when I remember that evening, I'm humbled again. (Note: It was my wife who first suggested we include this story in the book.)

As leaders, it's so easy to become full of ourselves. The Bible tells us that pride goes before a fall (sometimes literally!), but God gives grace to the humble. Thankfully, not all of life's lessons in this area are taught by a runaway yo-yo.

We have a saying in Texas: "Big hat, no cattle." That's something you don't want said about yourself. It's used to refer to someone who has a big head but no goods to support the image.

When you think of most leaders today—in politics, business, sports, and so on—*humility* is not likely to be at the top of the list of words you'd use to describe them. In fact, *humility* might not appear anywhere on the list. Can this really be a characteristic of a winning leader?

Well, think of all the leaders in recent years in almost every area of life, including religion, whose pride led them into terrible falls. Ethical failures, moral sellouts, financial crimes, lies to stockholders and judges and juries—these things have become the stuff of our daily headlines. It's not a pretty picture, nor is it worth the power or money possibly gained from such ventures.

That's why my whole premise for being a winning leader begins not with the size of your bank account or the number of employees on your payroll, but with the true definition of success: You walk with God as you rely on his promises, you love people, and you do work that you enjoy while you meet the needs of others or make their lives better.

If you're doing that last part—meeting needs or making lives better—chances are you'll have a healthy bank balance as well. But if you're not walking with God and loving people, piles of cash will offer only the coldest of comfort. Or, using the analogy above, you may have a lot of green "cattle," but they won't give you the things that make life worth living—peace of mind and heart, loving and respectful relationships, and a sense of purpose that goes well beyond putting big numbers on a spreadsheet.

I would go so far as to say that a leader who is not humble cannot be truly successful. But what does humility look like? And how can a leader cast the necessary vision for the staff and make the tough decisions without falling into what we might call the big-hat trap?

What Humility Is Not

Many people believe that a humble person is one with a lousy self-image, a self-described worm crawling through the dirt, or maybe even the dirt itself. You know the type: "I'm no good. I'm not as smart or good looking or successful as the other guy. It's no wonder that life doesn't give me any breaks." That's not humility at all. It's just poor self-esteem. It doesn't even square with the facts of life.

The truth is each and every person on this earth is an incredible creation of a loving God, made in his image. As the psalmist wrote, "I am fearfully and wonderfully made" (Ps. 139:14). Though our gifts and abilities vary, we have all been given the potential to love, do meaningful work, and make a positive difference in this world. In other words, we all have the capacity to be truly successful. To think of ourselves as worms is not only crippling in terms of trying to fulfill our potential, but also just plain wrong.

By the way, did you notice how the attitude of the "woe is me" individual is focused on self and not on others? The humble leader has a winning "there you are" mind-set as opposed to the self-serving "here I am" attitude. Being wrapped up in feelings of self-worthlessness is not humility at all. It's narcissism, plain and simple.

The First Facets of Humility

So what is humility? Think of it as a jewel with many facets. Each facet provides a slightly different perspective and is an essential part of the whole. The key facet is that focus on others. The humble person spends more time thinking of the needs and well-being of others rather than his or her own. In a given situation, the humble person thinks, *How can I help him or her?* rather than *What can I get for myself?*

This attitude is captured perfectly in the Scripture passage that says, "Do nothing out of selfish ambition or vain conceit, but in humility consider others better than yourselves. Each of you should look not only to your own interests, but also to the interests of others" (Phil. 2:3–4).

When I think of this aspect of humility, my mind turns to a wonderful woman named Betsy who ran the production side of my chocolate factory for a time. A wise and talented leader, she could be tough when the circumstances called for it, but she was always thinking of the welfare of the people who reported to her.

Each fall as stores built up inventory for the Christmas season, we would often get huge orders at the last minute. This usually meant that a lot of people had to work Saturdays and even Sundays, which were normally days off. Betsy, as the factory boss, could have set up the work schedules on Friday and enjoyed her weekends at leisure. After all, as long as an adequate number of managers were on hand and the work got done, she didn't have to be there. She could have figured, *I've put in my hours over the years. I've earned the right to relax. I've got good subordinates in place. I deserve my weekends off.*

Instead, her focus wasn't on "I." It was on others —both customers and those who worked for her. Her attitude was this: If my people have to work this weekend, I want to be there with them, helping them get the job done. I don't expect to be catered to; I'm here to support them.

Reflected in that brilliant facet of humility is another facet: The humble leader is willing to discipline himself for the good of the staff. It's easy to think and act as if you're above the rules that apply to others: You can come in late and leave early. You should have a reserved parking space. You deserve a private dining room, or at least the privilege of going to the head of the line in the company cafeteria. If you use equipment or make a mess somewhere, others can pick up after you.

You can imagine how that kind of attitude goes over with employees. Right—it doesn't! Instead of earning employees' respect and loyalty, resentment grows.

The humble leader, however, submits to the same rules and conditions as everyone else for the sake of morale. The true leader also is willing to do anything an employee would be asked to do—meaning he or she works at least as hard as anyone else or harder.

For instance, in my wife's cooking school, the crew uses a lot of kitchen tools: knives, spoons, measuring cups, whisks, and so on. Of course, all those tools have to be cleaned and put away after each class. It would be easy for Judie, as the busy owner, to leave that task entirely to students and employees, even for the tools she used. But Judie never does that. She made a rule early on that everyone is responsible to clean up his or her own mess and put away his or her own utensils. She submits to that rule along with everybody else. Both students and staff happily follow her example.

Do you see how one facet of humility in leadership reflects another? The humble leader thinks of employees, involves them and listens to them, and—still thinking of them—doesn't take himself too seriously.

Absolutely, work is serious, and meeting the needs of customers and employees is serious. But just as certainly, you have to be able to laugh at yourself along the way.

Remember my yo-yo incident? I could have let my pain and embarrassment turn into anger and frustration. I could have yelled at people to get them to stop laughing or gone off by myself and sulked. When I heard people joking about it in the office the next week, I could have glared at them and ordered them back to work.

Fortunately, by God's grace and with encouragement from Judie, I realized that what had happened was just plain funny. Though the humor was at my expense (in more ways than one), I had done a good job of setting myself up for the fall! With my cocky attitude and my prideful assumption that I could still do the trick as well as I could back when I was practicing it every day, I was almost bound to fail.

201

So I went with the flow. I laughed along with everyone else. I even retold the story myself, building it up by admitting how sure I had been of my ability in those fateful seconds before the accident. And I could tell, by the way people responded and things they said, that they respected me more, not less, for being able to laugh at myself.

That brings up one more sparkling facet of humility: The winning, humble leader seeks and is satisfied with internal accomplishments. Others don't see and applaud these things. In fact, awards typically are given for external results: increased sales, improved efficiency, new levels of community involvement.

What if companies began rewarding controlling temper under high pressure as highly as meeting any sales target? Or what if praise were given to the manager who encouraged people rather than sarcastically commenting on them?

While these might not be the sort of accomplishments to make headlines or be put up in lights, can you imagine the improvement they would make in your organization's morale?

Masterminding

As you exercise humility from the helm, your team will begin to shine—maybe not overnight, but in time. All the practices of humility, after all, help you become more open and willing to draw strength and insight from others—and then give them proper credit for the results that follow. This simple idea is called "masterminding."

I once heard the concept explained this way: Imagine a person's brain as a battery, with just so much capacity and energy to offer. The amount varies from one individual to another, but if you connect two batteries or brains so they work together, you get more output than if the two functioned separately. The principle follows that if you add more batteries or brains, the energy provided continues to increase above and beyond individual capacities.

In the supply chain for our chocolate factory, if we weren't getting a certain kind of chocolate in a timely fashion, we inevitably experienced slowdowns on the factory floor, as well as frustrated customers because orders promised by our sales staff couldn't be filled. I could have, like a big-hat leader, taken on the challenge of solving the problem by myself. *Who better than me to ride to the rescue?* I might think (imagining pats on the back from grateful employees).

Wrong. That's egotistical flattery.

A humble and wise leader would mastermind the problem: Call a meeting and invite the head of purchasing and the purchasing agents. Include the sharp assistant who's never encountered an unanswerable question or obstacle. Involve the guy from marketing who mentioned in a water cooler conversation that he'd read somewhere about bad weather in West Africa affecting the cocoa plant crop.

Together individuals on the team could compare notes for a fuller, richer picture than any one person could paint alone. Together the team would agree on who would look where for additional information. Together the team could go beyond brainstorming solutions to setting assignments and taking steps to resolve things.

Together the team could keep tabs on progress and address new issues along the way.

As the vital work of your team gets done faster, more effectively, and with more corporate passion, together you can celebrate—with kudos in the company newsletter, with bonuses for all the players, or with a corporate lunch or party with snacks. And always with better morale . . . in the end.

I saw this play out when our chocolate factory needed new facilities. We masterminded the design in the most grassroots way. Our vice president of operations, Tim, worked with an architect to draw up an initial proposal for our building's layout. Then we put those plans on a drafting table in my office and invited people to come by on their coffee breaks, look over the sketches, and offer any suggestions for improvements. Sally from the chocolate dipping room recommended moving the supply cabinets for easier access. Joe in shipping pointed out that more room was needed beside the loading docks for him to safely maneuver his forklift.

Soon we had scribbles all over the sketches. Post-it notes were attached at odd angles everywhere, and for a day or so we were inundated in more ideas than we ever expected. The input was valuable, proving that masterminding can get messy!

The mess leads to something better though. For us, it led to an incredibly designed facility that no industrial architect could have come up with on his or her own—or by meeting with just one or two of us. Another benefit: Everyone in our plant felt a sense of ownership in how things turned out, and that increased involvement, loyalty, and productivity.

Did you see another vital facet of humility in the masterminding idea? It's the willingness to share responsibilities and delegate. Look at it this way: If you're a bright, competent person, as most leaders are, it's easy to think you can do most any job better than anyone else, or at least in the best way, right? By that same logic, you can take all the credit when things turn out well.

You get the picture. Humble leaders see themselves not as the star of the show, but as the catalyst to help others get things done.

Frankly, this has been the toughest facet for me to accept, because I thought handing off work and letting others run with it meant I was slacking off to free up my time and energy. I struggled even more with giving up control. If I spent most of my time giving assignments, where was *my* sense of accomplishment at the end of the day?

Delegating and sharing responsibilities doesn't make you a slacker. It makes you smart and sets you apart from the micromanager who wastes a lot of time, attention, and energy on things that others could and should be doing. As a leader, you should be pursuing new business, rallying the team's focus on a common vision, and working on the things only you can do.

However, that doesn't necessarily mean barking out decisions, because another facet of the jewel called "humility" is to listen and hear. Many leaders tend to have strong opinions about everything, and they expect everyone in the room to agree with them. When someone starts expressing a view contrary to their own, these leaders want to jump right in and "straighten out" the variant thinking.

Likewise, I've seen many leaders who like to move through a meeting agenda in a brisk, businesslike fashion, keeping the discussion on track and moving. When someone starts to go down a bunny trail, the leader's instincts seem to scream "halt," and he steers the conversation as quickly as possible back to where, ahem, it ought to be.

Everyone has seen this before: Others are talking through a problem, while one antsy leader has already decided what should be done to solve it. As the discussion carries on, the leader begins to get extremely impatient and wants to grab the floor and announce a solution.

Of course, acting on such instinctive desires disrespects the person speaking and anyone else who might have another view. It not only short-circuits the process a group needs to make sure everyone is on board and feels ownership in the right decisions, but also squelches creativity and innovation. Sometimes a brilliant solution or new idea is just a comment away, and the leader without the humility to listen and hear can be poorer for his proud "efficiency."

For best success, learn when to bite your tongue and let others have their say. Look for ways to get everyone involved and contributing toward the common goal. You can be sure that blasting through the agenda, cutting conversation short, and forcing your will on everyone may save time in the short run, but in the long run it will cost you in hurt feelings and lost opportunities.

Tough Conversations

Yet another facet of humility blazes bright when you must have a tough conversation with someone. The circumstances can vary widely.

When I have to discipline an employee, for example, difficult—even painful—things have to be said. I could just hammer the employee with what he or she did wrong or how my expectations weren't met. But for a successful discussion, the winning leader humbles himself enough to think of standing in the employee's shoes: How would I best receive something difficult from a person in authority? How would I want to be treated? How could I be told the truth of the situation and yet still be shown respect? How could I be shown my short-comings and still leave the meeting feeling that the boss believes in me and my ability to get the job done?

As a leader, to handle the conversation honestly and also fairly and respectfully, that's what I need to do.

On the other hand, sometimes even as a leader you're on the receiving end of a tough conversation. Again, humility is required.

In the early days of our chocolate company, I made a lot of the sales calls on major accounts myself. I was trying to get our fine candies into a major department store, but the buyer was a hard case, to put it mildly. I would call to make an appointment, and she would hang up on me. Feeling angry and insulted, I had to cool down and swallow my pride before calling her back.

Eventually, through sheer persistence, I got an appointment (the first, but not the last). But even then, as I sat in her office, she would take a call in the middle of my presentation or get up and walk out of the room! At least once or twice, she didn't even bother to come back. Talk about tough conversations! It took all the humility and self-control I could muster, along with some quick prayers for patience and grace, to remain calm and polite.

Success, in this case, came when the woman asked one day, "Would you like to be in our mail order catalog?" That represented a huge step forward for our company.

A final facet of humility should be seen in the way we speak every day. I've seen any number of leaders who are obviously trying to impress people by using the biggest words they can find in the dictionary. These people also tend to put others down, take all the credit for the accomplishments of their teams, and shift the blame for their own shortcomings onto others.

As leaders, we need the humility to speak plainly, say exactly what we mean, tell the truth, and show common courtesy to everyone we meet. That includes saying please and thank you, giving credit where credit is due, and taking responsibility for our own mistakes.

In the Face of Losses

Sometimes as leaders we don't need to work at staying humble. Life's circumstances do a very good job of keeping our egos in check. For example, the simple fact is that many factors that affect the success of our enterprises are entirely beyond our control. We must accept that fact and remain flexible, adjusting our plans as the changing tides demand.

Regulatory changes. Cultural changes. New offers from competitors. New technologies. Demographic changes. These are just some of the external conditions that can change at any time, forcing us to trash the best laid plans.

In the 1980s, for instance, our chocolate company was heavy into bulk chocolate. Department stores had their own candy counters and would sell chocolate by the piece or by the pound. We would ship our product in five-pound bulk boxes to the stores, where it would be displayed under glass and sold one piece at a time.

We foresaw a big future for this kind of sale, and all of our research confirmed that people mainly wanted the fine chocolates. They were willing to pay for the goods but didn't want to pay extra for additional trappings. That sounded good to us—it saved us the effort and expense of designing and buying those fancy boxes, ribbons, decals, and such.

By the middle of the decade, however, the market began to shift. Fine chocolates were now being bought not just to satisfy a customer's craving, but also as gifts or for special occasions. That meant customers wanted their chocolates in nice boxes. Department stores were beginning to respond by phasing out their candy counters and ordering fancy boxed chocolates instead of bulk chocolate.

This change in demand was entirely outside our control. As well as we thought we had foreseen and prepared for the future of our market, we were just plain wrong. The reality of the situation literally sent us back to the drawing board, humbled, to start designing new boxes and marketing campaigns.

If a product or campaign isn't working, you had better be on top of the numbers enough and in close enough contact with your customers to catch on to the fact as quickly as possible. Then, when the trend is clear, the reality inescapable, you can't let pride or emotion stand in the way of what needs to be done. You need to cut your losses and move on.

Part of the moving on is to do a critique session (we called these "postmortem" sessions—sort of a business autopsy on what happened). This, too, requires the willingness to eat some humble pie as hard truths are examined: What went wrong? Were some assumptions faulty? Did we rely too much on intuition and not enough on research? Were there product problems? Off-target marketing? Delivery issues? Failure to listen to our customers?

The good news is that if we can accept and even respect the things we can't control, we can stop wasting time bemoaning the changes and get creative about finding ways to turn them into opportunities.

For our chocolate company, the swing to boxing fine chocolates gave us an opportunity to show what made us unique and set ourselves apart from our competitors—something unmarked chocolates sitting in a display case could never do.

Spiritual Resources

There's more good news in the fact that rich spiritual resources are available to help us stay humble in the healthiest sense. To begin with, being in relationship with God gives us a sense of worth and purpose. And if we know that we're "fearfully and wonderfully made," of priceless worth to the one who made us, it's a lot easier to rise above the self-seeking attitude of pride and put others first.

It's also much easier to admit when we've made mistakes, to scrap pet plans, to give someone else the spotlight, to resist beating out the competition at any cost, and to take every other action that's necessary but runs counter to the way most people define success.

If we're in tune with God's Spirit, we can also seek strength and guidance from him to do the right thing. The Bible says that God accomplishes things through us "not by might nor by power, but by [his] Spirit" (Zech. 4:6).

When I manage to be humble in the face of the temptation to be prideful—when I can admit my shortcomings or put the needs and desires of others ahead of my own—it's usually because I've been praying about the situation and I sense the prompting and the energizing of the Spirit to do what I know I should.

I'm more likely to be praying and open to the Spirit's prompting when I'm regularly having what we call a "quiet time"—just a few minutes at the start of the day to read the Bible and talk with God about my concerns. It is amazing how much better my frame of mind is later in the day, when challenges come along, if I've begun things that way.

Corporate Pride

The temptation to be prideful isn't just something that afflicts us as individual leaders. When things are going well for the firm—sales are strong, the product or service is good, customers are happy, market share is growing—it's easy for the entire leadership team, or even the whole organization, to take on a swagger and think it can do no wrong.

The Enron Corporation was known for that kind of pride. Although many issues contributed to its downfall, pride was at the root. Enron leaders believed that

211

they could do anything they wanted, break any rule, and get away with it. That's pride taken to the extreme of arrogance.

When things are going well and the organization seems to be running like a well-oiled machine, you need to remember the mistakes made along the way, the many people whose contributions have been vital, and the hard work still ahead. You also need to remember that it's the customers who determine your success. Without their willingness to buy what you have to offer, none of your efforts or supposed brilliance amount to a hill of beans.

There's another kind of corporate pride sometimes called the "edifice complex." When companies are prospering, or they just want to make a "statement" to the business world, they like to build big, bold, beautiful facilities. They then fill them with the latest and best in furnishings, machines, and office equipment.

The problem with the edifice complex, even if the firm doesn't go deeply into debt to finance it, is that those lovely new buildings may soon be outgrown if the business continues to thrive. And for sure, all that expensive equipment will soon grow obsolete as technology continues to advance.

Pride says, "We want to build it and own it." Humility says, "Maybe we'd be better off just leasing facilities and equipment. Then, when needs change or better tools come along, we aren't saddled with obsolete buildings and machines." Obsolescence is the owner's problem; by leasing, you can have the latest equipment all the time at no additional expense and without having to sell off the old "stuff."

The Nike sports equipment and clothing company has learned the value of not having to own everything. Nike owns no factories and no machines for manufacturing its shoes or golf clubs or anything else it sells. What it has, instead of a lot of real estate, is an extensive network of suppliers that it calls "production partners."

The public thinks of Nike as a manufacturer. And it does indeed "make" and sell all kinds of equipment, clothes, shoes, and boots for almost every sport. Its swoosh logo has become one of the best-known trademarks in the world. Yet it is, in fact, what we might call a virtual company. It's really a research and design studio attached to a great marketing department.

What's the best approach for your organization? Is it owning everything? Leasing? Working with a network of production partners? Some combination of these options? Or something else altogether?

As a leader, it's your responsibility to make such choices as objectively and honestly as possible in terms of what's good for your organization—not in terms of what would be most satisfying to the individual or corporate ego.

The Humble Salesperson

Finally, let me say a few words about the specific kinds of humility required of successful salespeople.

First, every bit as much as a corporate president, a salesperson has to put the needs of others ahead of his or her own needs. The sales rep who goes into a customer meeting thinking about how he's going to push something onto the customer and so meet his quota for the month is both arrogant and destined to fail before he ever opens his mouth to begin the presentation.

On the other hand, the sales rep who seeks to help satisfy the customer's best interests will walk out a winner every time—even when a sale isn't made that particular day.

I'm reminded of the wonderful old movie *Miracle on 34th Street,* most of which takes place in Macy's department store in New York City. One Christmas season, an elderly gentleman is hired to play the store Santa, and he takes a most unusual approach to the job.

The store Santa is supposed to encourage the children who come to sit on his lap to request toys sold by Macy's. And when what the kids want isn't carried by Macy's, the department manager tells him to steer their attention to things Macy's *does* offer.

Well, much to that manager's chagrin, this new Santa doesn't play along. Not only does he not try to redirect the kids' interest to toys carried by Macy's, but he even tells them and their parents what other stores they can shop to find what they want! He goes so far as to recommend Gimbel's department store—Macy's archrival in New York retailing!

The manager is appalled. Not only is his new Santa not doing as instructed, but he's an outright traitor. The manager is prepared to fire his Santa that very day.

And then an interesting thing starts to happen. Mr. Macy, the store owner, begins getting letters from customers. "Thank you," they all say in so many words, "for hiring a store Santa who puts the happiness of our children ahead of sales. We've never seen such a thing before, but we appreciate it! You can count on us to be faithful Macy's shoppers!"

By caring more about the customers' needs than immediate sales, this Santa actually increased Macy's business and enhanced the store's reputation in the community.

Second, the successful salesperson must avoid the *false* humility that keeps him or her from asking for the order at the end of the presentation. Underperforming salespeople might say, "I didn't want to be pushy," or "The buyer wasn't showing much enthusiasm, so I figured he was only going to say no anyway."

That mind-set isn't humility; it's cowardice. If a salesperson doesn't believe in the product or service he's selling, he ought to quit and find a line of work he can pursue with integrity. But if a sales rep *does* believe that his product or service *will* help the customer, he should present it with enthusiasm and not hesitate to try to close the deal.

Sometimes, for any number of possible reasons, the customer will say no. That can be tough to handle emotionally, but it comes with the job. And the simple fact is that unless you ask the question, you'll rarely make a sale.

So have confidence in your product, present it well, and ask for the sale. Never let false humility get in your way.

&

The truly successful leader is a humble leader. And lessons in humility are often learned through painful experience. My hope is that you will benefit from what I've been through and not have to repeat my mistakes.

Don't let pride bring you down. Stay humble and see if life doesn't have a way of lifting you up.

Can You Taste Success?

1. What is the state of your self-esteem? On what do you base it?
2. Which facet of humility do you most need to develop? Why? How can you begin to do that in the next week?
3. Think of a time when your organization may have been guilty of corporate pride. What were the results of that attitude?
4. How good are you at handling losses emotionally? Spiritually? With your behavior? What one step can you make in each area to move closer to where you want to be in handling disappointments or failures? (Make the steps small and measurable, and once you take them think of a next step that moves you closer to your goal.)
5. How strong are your spiritual resources in helping you stay humble as a leader? What can you do to strengthen them?

A FINAL WORD

SUCCESS THAT LASTS

Wall Street, the popular and Oscar-winning movie, tells the story of a young stockbroker in New York named Bud Fox. Bud is fairly new to the business, and he's eager to get ahead. He figures that the best way to do that is to "bag the elephant"—to land as a client a highly success-ful corporate raider named Gordon Gekko. (You may remember Gekko's famous line from the film: "Greed is good.")

In an attempt to obtain an appointment with the busy and important Gekko, Bud calls his office every day for months on end. He never gets through to "The Man." Finally, on Gekko's birthday, Bud shows up at his office with a present, a box of expensive and hard-to-get Cuban cigars. "May I present the gift to Mr. Gekko personally?" Bud begs the secretary.

Admiring his persistence and taking pity, she tells him to have a seat and wait. She'll see if Mr. Gekko will squeeze him in at some point in the day.

Bud ends up spending the entire morning in the waiting room. Finally, however, his tenacity is rewarded. Mr. Gekko will see him for a few minutes after all.

As Bud stands and straightens his tie, preparing himself mentally for this key meeting, he says to himself, "Life all comes down to a few moments. This is one of them."

For Bud Fox, that first meeting does, indeed, prove to be pivotal. It starts him down a path of ethical compromise and outright corruption. At the end of the trail is the strong likelihood of a prison cell.

For most of us leaders, though, true success is not about what we do in a handful of moments spread across a lifetime. Real and lasting success is about the things we do and say, and the way we say and do them, day in and day out. It's about the things we've explored in this book:

- The way we communicate with others in the organization
- How we treat people
- The values we stand for and behind
- Giving our best effort every day and not taking people or results for granted
- Earning credibility and the right to be followed
- Welcoming small failures on the often difficult path of testing new ideas and eventually reaching tomorrow's breakthroughs

In short, true success grows out of consistently doing these things, even when we're tired or frustrated. It results from disciplining ourselves to do what we know is right in a given situation, even when other, easier-looking options appear to offer temporary solutions.

Help Wanted—and Needed

As I've said often throughout this book, however, doing these right things often doesn't come naturally to us. We *do* get tired. We grow proud. We become complacent. Our negative emotions get the better of us, rather than the other way around.

In short, we need help doing the right things.

As I've also said, that help is available through God's Spirit living in us and producing his fruit in our lives. In the Book of Galatians, we read, "The fruit of the Spirit is love, joy, peace, patience, kindness, goodness, faithfulness, gentleness and self-control" (5:22–23)—the traits underlying each of the habits described in this book.

That's where we get the power to be truly successful leaders. God's Spirit gives us the will and the strength to do and say the right things, even when we'd rather not. And that's why I had to say more about him at this point. Not to do so would be like telling you how to build a smooth-running car engine without also telling you about gasoline. And even a Ferrari without gas is just a big, fancy block of metal.

"The mind controlled by the Spirit is life and peace," we read in the Book of Romans (8:6). "It is God who works in you to will and to act according to his good purpose," we see in Philippians (2:13).

As we submit to his leadership in our lives, we can know true success, not only in leading an organization, but also in every other area of our existence. We can experience every bit of the love, joy, peace, patience, kindness, goodness, faithfulness, gentleness, and self-control listed in the Galatians passage.

We can, in short, enjoy life as it was meant to be by the God who made and loves us all.

THE 12 PROVEN HABITS

1. *Make sure everyone's talking.*
   —Teach respect, encourage feedback (even when it hurts), and listen carefully in order to respond and direct; then see how these steps cycle and communication flows so the organization can grow.
2. *Lead rather than manage.*
   —Focus your time and energy on doing the right things rather than on doing less important things right.
3. *Keep everyone on the same path.*
   —Set an example, love those you're leading, and go out of your way to help them be winners, too.
4. *Put good work ahead of money.*
   —Love winning a customer or supporter as much as, if not more than, earning a buck.
5. *Always think of the core customer.*
   —Beware of the excitement at the dance overriding who you brought there.

6. *Don't try to go it alone.*
   —Remember all the colors and textures it takes to paint the big picture.
7. *Never rest on your laurels.*
   —Choose consistency over flash, do your homework, prepare—and then some—and read to lead.
8. *Earn credibility every day.*
   —Put people first and you'll be more than a leader in name only.
9. *Welcome small failures.*
   —Mistakes can be stepping-stones to new discoveries—and business, support, and reach.
10. *Pursue new ideas, no matter how heavy the current demands.*
    —The world and markets constantly change, so you'd better find today the ideas that will be tomorrow's products and/or services.
11. *Let passion fuel your work.*
    —Loving what you do gets you through the tough days and inspires those who labor with you.
12. *Embrace the power of humility.*
    —Real leaders know how to ride to the rescue, do what needs to be done, and serve others—to serve the organization best.

Bill Byrd, owner of the Byrd Group in Fort Worth, Texas, helps small companies to build new markets, cut expenses, and turn around their businesses when they're struggling with declining market share, low cash flow, and other challenges. For information about how Bill can help your firm or about having him speak to your firm or church, visit his web site: www.byrdgroup.com.

Judie Byrd, owner of the Culinary School of Fort Worth, which is mentioned a number of times in this book, can be reached at www.judiebyrd.com. Her school offers hands-on classes, demonstration classes, and a Chef Pro course for those who want to become culinary professionals.

Larry K. Weeden, who directs the editorial team for Focus on the Family Publishing, has assisted such leading communicators as Gary Smalley, Josh McDowell, Frank Minirth, and Jay Kesler with their writing. He enjoys helping people who have a solid message to express themselves clearly and effectively.